And
DAVID PERCEIVED
HE WAS KING

IDENTITY - the Key to Your DESTINY

DALE L. MAST

DEDICATION

I dedicate this book to the "David" that is in you through Jesus Christ, the seed of David. May the call of God and the dream He has placed in your heart empower you to journey through the traumas of life to the place of authority and fruitfulness that Father God has purposed and prepared for you.

I thank God for my wife, LuAnne, who has supported me in this endeavor. Her amazing walk with God has always inspired me to go deeper with God. I am so blessed to have her pastor Destiny Christian Church with me as well as traveling nationally and internationally. I am thankful for our children: Michael, Benjamin, Matthew, Heidi, Andrew & Amanda and Zachary & Amber; grandchildren Bailey and Lena.

I honor Pastor Millard Benner who inspired me as a young boy to love God. I honor my parents, Lawrence & Carolyn Mast, who inspired me in so many ways to live for God. I honor Bishop Bill and Evelyn "Mom" Hamon, our spiritual parents, who gave me a greater understanding of God and what He desired to accomplish through man.

I thank the extended Destiny Christian Church family that has encouraged me since 1983 when I became a pastor at thirty years old.

I honor Father God as the foundation of everything I am and ever hope to be, one of His sons.

Dale L. Mast

Contact Information for
Speaking Engagements
Dale L Mast
2161 Forrest Ave
Dover, DE 19904
dalemast@aol.com
destinydover.org
302-674-4288

FOREWORDS

I have used Dale Mast's book, "And David Perceived He Was King", to help provide keen insight and wisdom for businessmen, recording artists, worship leaders, pastors, students and many others around the world who are seeking to find or expand their kingdom purpose. I have personally experienced and witnessed the deep personal transformation, expansions and fulfillment of life dreams and callings as readers applied the principles taught. Each chapter contains detailed prophetic applications from David's life story that help provide a clearer more vivid picture of the Father's heart to influence and direct every person into their life purpose and destiny.

Emerging leaders will love the spiritual foundation the book provides, experienced leaders will enjoy a new awareness of the importance of one's personal identity, mentoring leaders will want to use the book to develop the next generation of leaders. All who read the book will benefit from its wisdom. If you're looking for some encouraging help to adjust or shift you, your family, or team into new mindsets for Kingdom leadership, it's in your hands.

Rocky Tannehill

Entrepreneur and Business Consultant

Dale Mast has done a masterful job of presenting some life-transforming truths in his new book, "*And David Perceived He Was King.*" His revelation and keen insight concerning "identity" as the key to progressively advancing in your maturity and ministry is enlightening, encouraging, and enabling.

In my sixty-one years of ministry, I have read numerous books and have written scores of forewords for other authors. Not all of them added new truth to my accumulation of knowledge. This book by Dale Mast added new insights and encouragement to my life. David has always been my main biblical character after God told me, when I started pastoring at the age of nineteen, that my life would be patterned after David's. I have read and preached sermons on David, but Dale brings out applicable truths that I had not seen before, but could relate to them as I read his manuscript.

You will be enlightened and abundantly blessed as you read this book and appropriate the wonderful truths presented. You just may find the missing link to your greater success and ultimate fulfillment of God's purpose for your life. Read this book carefully and intently, and the Holy Spirit will illuminate and relate these vital truths to your life and ministry. God bless you, Dale, for your revelation, and for taking the time to make it known to the Body of Christ, the Church.

Dr. Bill Hamon

Bishop: Christian International Apostolic Network

Author: *The Eternal Church; Prophets & Personal Prophecy; The Prophetic Movement; Prophetic Principles; Apostles & Prophets; The Day of the Saints; Seventy Reasons For Speaking in Tongues; Prophetic Scriptures Yet to be Fulfilled: During The Third and Final Reformation; Who Am I & Why Am I Here?; How Can These Things Be?*

A nd David Perceived He Was King is incredibly refreshing. This is a "must read before you proceed" book! Pause whatever else you've got going on, get out your highlighter and pencil and read this book now. Trust me, the immediate impact that this book offers you is profound.

As a son, husband and father, and also as a physician, CEO and entrepreneur, this book is a game changer. If you're in business, read this book. I have launched new businesses and new products since reading this book and the upgrade has been remarkable because of the revelation packed within. Knowing your true identity is truly the key ingredient to experiencing transformation, understanding value, fulfilling your purpose, realizing your destiny and living in greater freedom in business and life!

I have shared this book with dozens of colleagues, physicians, CEO's, friends, and given it as a gift to my staff, family and friends... and the positive feedback resounds! They have told me it is among the top books they've read, if not the top. It is priceless!

Dr. Peter Camiolo

Physician, Soul Adjuster

Founder of Chiro-CEO

Live IN Alignment!

www.chiro-ceo.com

www.linkedin.com/in/petercamiolo/

www.facebook.com/drpetercamiolo/

Work From Rest | Prosper In Business | Enjoy Your Life

Like Dale Mast, I have always been very fascinated with King David's life. I have studied his life more than that of any other Bible character other than Jesus, contemplating his highs and lows, victories and failures, losses and gains. David lived in caves and palaces; he was celebrated one day, rejected and exiled the next. This leader was an adulterer, yet was still referred to as a "man after God's heart." I'm glad God keeps it real in scripture, airing the dirty laundry as well as the clean — it gives hope to the rest of us not-so-perfect mortals. What a life this man lived.

As I have read David's story over the years, I've often found myself thinking how much I would enjoy an even deeper study of his life, but just never seemed to find the time. It was obvious to me that there was so much more insight and revelation hidden in this man's life than what I had already gleaned.

I just found a big chunk of it!

This book is a treasure. The insights the Holy Spirit has shared with us through Dale Mast are extraordinary. So many Christian books are filled with facts and information that make us a little smarter—but no different. Not so with this book. The truth it contains, if taken seriously and applied, will change you—*guaranteed!*

I understand well the importance of us finding our identity in God, and the debilitating effect it has on one when this isn't the case. For instance, I grew up a very insecure person, filled with fears of rejection and failure. This shaped my personality far more than I realized and, like all who deal with these issues, I had subconsciously formed many coping actions and reactions. These responses became so natural that I lived life through a façade—and didn't even realize it! When the Lord was finally able to bring healing to me, my entire personality changed.

Several things contributed to my insecurities. One of them occurred when I was ten years old. My Sunday School class engaged in a scripture memorization program in which each child was responsible to memorize a verse or two; on the big Sunday we were to go in front of the entire congregation and recite our verses. When it was my turn, stage fright set in, my mind went blank, and I couldn't remember my verse. The pastor, seated in the front row, began to prod me: "Come on boy. What's the matter with you?" This only made it worse.

I wished for some help—just a word or two to get me started—but none came. My panic increased, and as it did,

I grew very embarrassed and began to cry. The pastor, now angry, said with disgust and sarcasm, "Get off the stage, boy."

That pastor was my dad.

Over the years my dad and I became very close. He dealt with many of his own identity issues, and throughout my ministry was one of my greatest supporters. But it is impossible to overestimate the effect that day had on me. Until I was twenty-one years old, I couldn't stand in front of people and talk. I wouldn't give oral book reports, address my class in school, or deliver any kind of public address. I simply couldn't. Regardless of how hard I tried, when I stood in front of people to talk, my mind would go blank.

But when I was twenty-one, God began reshaping my identity. He brought healing to my damaged psyche, peeling back layer after layer of wrong thinking and damaged emotions. Then He began rebuilding my identity around the security of knowing Him as my loving and accepting Father. The transformation was amazing—I felt like a new person, and in many ways, I was. Over the years the process of forming my identity in Christ has continued, and it seems that in every phase of my life a new aspect of who He created me to be is revealed... exactly as it occurred with King David.

In many ways, I stumbled into my healing. I was fortunate to be around the right people, and as a Bible school student had massive amounts of time to read the scriptures and pray. Through those times, and with good input, God's love broke through. But you don't have to "stumble into" your healing or the awesome future He has planned for you. There are principles to follow that will make it easier to find out who you were created to be and what you were created to do.

You're holding a great resource for this in your hand. I'm always amazed when a person like Dale can take concepts, which seem so ethereal and mystical to most of us, and break them down into understandable bite-size pieces. Yet, that is exactly what he has done for us on the subject of forming our identity in Christ, and fulfilling our God-given purpose.

Regardless of your level of spiritual understanding, life will make more sense as you read this book. The ways of God will enlighten and guide you in new ways, leading you out of the fog and into clear skies. You'll understand yourself more, which is profoundly important, and you'll also receive a new grid for processing life's experiences. Simply stated, you'll become more of the "you" God imagined when He decided He needed you on the planet. And that, my friend, is a game changer.

Enjoy.

Dutch Sheets

Author: *The Power of Hope; Becoming Who You Are; God's Timing for Your Life, The Pleasure of His Company; Intercessory Prayer; Dream; Authority in Prayer; The Beginner's Guide to Intercessory Prayer; Watchman Prayer; Releasing the Prophetic Destiny of a Nation; Redeeming the Time; How to Pray for Lost Loved Ones; Getting in God's Face: The River of God*

Sh **D**ale Mast's new book "And David Perceived He Was King" on identity being the key to our destiny is foundational and profound for Christian business leaders! As a businessman and investor, I have had the privilege of consulting many small business leaders and Christian CEO's.

I had been hot on this trail of upgrading identity to sonship since 2008. This new book is the best that I have found and it's worthy of multiple reads! There's no fluff in Dale's writings. The reader will find many revelational treasures that will cause them to pause and process at the deepest levels of their own heart! If they get this book and take that challenge... it will start upgrades of identity for many seasons to come... they absolutely will never be the same person!
Terry Tyson
www.PartneringWithFather.com
Entrepreneur, Businessman and Consultant

Every Christian should read this captivating and compelling book about King David's journey to the throne. From the very first chapter, I could identify with the struggles and battles he personally endured. I found encouragement and hope for the future as I turned each page.

The faithfulness of God is unmistakable and it ministers encouragement to every believer to continue to dream your God dream. This is a book you cannot put down because it speaks to you so personally. I wholeheartedly endorse and recommend "And David Perceived He Was King" as a "must read" for every Christian. I loved the book!

Bishop Anne Gimenez

Rock Ministerial Fellowship

Author: *Born to Preach; Marking Your Children for God; The Emerging Christian Woman; Resurrection Life Now!*

I met Dale, and his wife, LuAnne, several years ago. I was immediately struck with the thought, "Here is a man with a clear prophetic gift and a compassionate pastor's heart." The more time my wife and I have been privileged to spend with them has only deepened our appreciation of them and our trust in them. Our church family has also benefitted greatly from their ministry. They truly are servants of the Lord who humbly walk in a powerful anointing.

As you read this book, your heart will be touched. Dale's insights into the life of David—"a man after the heart of God"—will stir your heart to pursue God's heart too. Just as David discovered his true identity in the presence of the Lord, you will be moved to do the same. As a pastor, I have met all types of leaders over the years. Dale is among those I have come to love and trust. So, I encourage you to receive his ministry in the pages of this book. Your time spent here will be well worth it!

Blessings to you, my friend.

Dave Hess

Senior Pastor of Christ Community Church

Author: *Hope Beyond Disappointment; Hope Beyond Reason*

Dale Mast is a teacher/activator at our Global School, which activates students in the supernatural gifts of the Holy Spirit. He is a favorite teacher and much loved by our students and staff. His new book, *"And David Perceived He Was King,"* is an excellent resource with so much practical insight on the journey to be used of God.

It not only deals with the call of God, but also addresses the needed process to enter it. Our identity is the key to become what God calls us to do. I highly recommend Dale and his new book.

Blessings,

Randy Clark, D. Min.

Founder and President of Global Awakening and the Apostolic Network of Global Awakening

Author: *The Essential Guide to the Power of the Holy Spirit; There is More!; Finding Victory When Healing Doesn't Happen; The Essential Guide to Healing; The Biblical Guidebook to Deliverance; Lighting Fires; Baptism in the Holy Spirit; Open Heaven—Are You Thirsty? Healing Unplugged; Ministry Team Training Manual; Learning to Minister Under the Anointing*

You will be very blessed as you read this book about David. It will impact your life and identity. My husband has an incredible gift to teach and bring revelation from the Word of God. I love the life of David. He faced many challenges and overcame them. He was a warrior who wasn't afraid to confront the enemy. He was overlooked by his father, ridiculed by his oldest brother, and faced many traumas through life.

This book reveals David's journey to establish his true identity as he moved from the fields to the throne room. It will help you shatter the lies of the enemy that every person must break. Dale and I travel nationally and internationally, teaching and ministering to many people. His teachings on David's life have impacted many people, including me. Dale's book will help you enter your destiny as you live as a true son, without shame.

I thank God for bringing Dale into my life. You can read how God supernaturally brought us together and restored both of our lives in my book, *"God, I Feel Like Cinderella!"*

Love you, Dale.

LuAnne Mast

Senior Pastor at Destiny Christian Church

Eagle Fire Ministries

Author: *God, I Feel Like Cinderella*

destinydover.org

eaglefireministries.org

302-674-4288

Books by Dale Mast

And David Perceived He Was King
Two Sons and a Father
The Throne of David

CONTENTS

—⌘—

INTRODUCTION

For years, I have studied the intriguing life of David to understand the keys crucial to every believer's life. God chose to showcase David's life to give us insight into man's relationship with Him. It is His invitation into intimacy with Him as we pursue our destiny and His purposes on the earth. One day as I was reading the Bible, these words stood out to me: "And David perceived he was king."

> *"And **David perceived** that the Lord had established him king over Israel, and that he had exalted his kingdom for his people Israel's sake" (2 Sam. 5:12, KJV).*

The Holy Spirit was drawing me to explore this transition in David's thinking. If David suddenly perceived that the Lord had established him as king over Israel, it also reveals that he didn't perceive it. The crown was resting on his head and the people were calling him King David, but he didn't fully comprehend that the Lord had established him as king of Israel.

David's internal struggle seemed so clear in this verse. I knew there was a powerful key hidden in that verse. I began rethinking David's journey to the throne. If he could defeat Goliath when the entire army was frozen in fear, why would becoming king be so difficult for this man of great faith?

I always thought of David as a gifted leader who experienced unusual favor from God and man. David was a worshipper who knew how to trust God and experienced the victories of Heaven. He overcame many integrity challenges with amazing grace. I never considered that David struggled with his identity. I always viewed him as a confident leader. He seemed like a born winner, moving from one victory to another.

David had been king over Judah for seven and a half years when Israel's elders came to him at Hebron and anointed him to be king over all Israel. David and his men marched to Jerusalem and defeated the mocking Jebusites—who had occupied this part of Israel before Joshua's conquest until the time of David. Even so, David still didn't fully grasp that he was established as the king of Israel.

These issues concerning identity are very normal for every person. This is a shared experience for those who choose to yield their life to God to become what He has determined. To live out a "God dream" requires many shifts to stay in pursuit of that vision. The enemy will attack you strategically to stop your mind from shifting into your future, but God knows the plans He has to prosper you—the plans He has to bring you hope and a future.

Why did David struggle to perceive that he was king? What caused him to shift? These are questions that I will be addressing in this book. What helped him shift into his new season will help shift you into yours. You must possess each new season to fulfill your destiny. It is much like climbing a ladder—each rung is very important.

It took faith for David to defeat Goliath. Yet, identity was required to take the throne. Faith brought David victory, but identity would be needed to fulfill his destiny. Faith believes what God can do—identity believes what God can do through you. God brings peace—that's our faith in His ability, but can He bring peace through you? That is identity!

The purpose of this book is to help you step into the fullness of your identity to complete your assignments from heaven. Until David "perceived" that he was king, his activities didn't fully match up with his destiny. When you perceive your new position in life, your goals, purposes, and activities will shift as you enter your "new" season.

If you don't fully embrace your present identity, you will block, delay, or hinder what God has called you to do. Your life will not be as effective or fruitful as it possibly could be. You must fulfill your destiny to help others enter theirs.

Are you stuck in the past because of hurt, disappointment, or partial success? Have you given up on parts of your dreams or destiny because of the traumatic, devaluing events that you endured? Have so many things been taken from your life that you have started to wonder if there really is anything that is yours to possess and enjoy?

Don't give up one iota of the destiny that God put inside of you! It's time to dream again. It's time to "re-vision" your life. It's your time to enter a "new" season. Carry the dream until the dream carries you!

Dale Mast
Facebook Dale Mast
dalemast@aol.com
eaglefireministries.org
destinydover.org
302-674-4288

Chapter One

A LIFE SHIFT REQUIRES AN IDENTITY SHIFT

"The word of the Lord came to me, saying, 'Before I formed you in the womb I knew you, before you were born I set you apart; I appointed you as a prophet to the nations.' 'Ah, Sovereign Lord,' I said, 'I do not know how to speak; I am only a child.' **But the Lord said to me, 'Do not say, "I am only a child"'"** *(Jer. 1:4–7). Composite of Translations*

Whenever God visited a man in the scriptures, it was the end of one season and at the beginning of another one. Identity shifts are required for each new season. In each new season, we must see God with a greater level of clarity. We are also required to see ourselves in a new way. Increased responsibilities are naturally connected to a new identity. Our relationship with Him shifts as well. New honor is given to release a new realm of authority and identity. It coincides with the new purpose and new activities of the new season of life we have entered. Did I say "new"?

If Ford, General Motors, and Dodge can do *new* every year, then God can certainly do *new* every day! *New* has a smell to it. When we sit in a brand-new car, we notice it has a unique smell a used car doesn't have. *Old* has a smell as well. His mercies are new every morning to create new within us. If His mercies were new at the end of the day, the main purpose would be to forgive sin. We all know His mercies take away sin, but we also need to understand that His new mercies are available to guide us through each day with fresh insights to experience a new day. His new mercies break us out of the old patterns into new ways that give entrance to our new season.

At the very core of any destiny shift, there must be an identity shift. The way we see ourselves is crucial to our destiny. We can't see ourselves correctly until the Father speaks to us. It takes a father to reveal a son. He will also reveal things that we can no longer speak about ourselves so that we can shift into our future with Him. God knows that what we think and say about ourselves is so central to His call on our lives. Until we speak what He has spoken about us, we will not impact the earth with heaven.

In each shift we must have a clear understanding of what has been deleted, de-emphasized, redefined, strengthened, and birthed in us for our new season. A new identity forces out the limitations and needed restrictions of a past season.

An identity shift accelerates us into destiny. Confidence and clarity are required to walk in God's dream for our lives. It takes the new to move out the old. The old doesn't leave because we are tired of it—old only leaves when the new displaces it. The new starts with what we say about ourselves. God is preparing a new season for us by changing the way we speak about ourselves. Our words create our identity.

For many years as I traveled to the nations, I referred to myself as "a voice to shift Christians in the nations," rather than "a voice to shift the nations." One day I heard the Lord speak to me. He said, "I do not agree with you." I recognized that I wasn't allowed to speak those words anymore. It took two years to clear my spirit of that mindset so that I could extend my faith to impact a nation.

I was getting ready to travel to Burma (or Myanmar) in 2008. I asked God to reveal my identity as a voice to the nations on this trip. At the last meeting in Burma, there was an unusual presence of the Lord and He instructed me to give Pastor Mung a ring—it would be a "Joseph ring" of authority to his nation. As I placed the "Joseph ring" on his hand—these words came to me, "Pastor Mung, God is going to make you like Joseph to this nation." He chuckled to himself, "How could this ever happen since Christians are so persecuted?" Christians had been oppressed for years; others had even been martyred in the remote villages.

Two weeks after we left, a typhoon devastated the city. Yet none of Pastor Mung's 8,000 church members had died.

As he was providing his people with food and meeting their physical needs, the "Joseph" word came back to him. He decided to focus on helping the people of his nation. Pastor Mung began to offer food and medical help to the same people who had thrown sticks and bricks at his church during their worship services.

Word got out about what he was doing, and major ministries from around the world started sending him money. Millions of dollars came in over the next six months allowing him to distribute vast amounts of food—just like Joseph. A wealthy Hindu man who mistrusted his own leaders gave him money and commended him for a job well done. Pastor Mung led a team of seventy-four doctors to help the Hindus affected by the typhoon. A Hindu priest told him, "If this would have happened to the Christians, we wouldn't have helped you. Why are you helping us?" Then, they opened up their temples for his medical teams to provide medical aid and to distribute food. Of his team of seventy-four doctors, only four were Christians—the rest were Hindu!

The government gave him unprecedented freedom in helping with the rebuilding process. It was the favor of Joseph. He laughed with joy as he told me the story. It was unbelievable! God had to stop my words to shift my identity so I could speak words to shift his identity to impact his nation.

Years earlier, I was invited to speak in India by my uncle, Dr. Bill Mast. He had traveled the nations for decades on medical mission trips and was now holding crusades. He wanted me to speak to the Indian pastors. A decade prior, he had moved to the other side of the county and we hadn't really kept in touch. As such, it was a bit unexpected when he said, "Dale, I was praying about whom to invite on this trip—and it really surprised me when God brought your face before me." It surprised me as well, but I did not take it to heart.

The meeting of three hundred pastors grew to a thousand. During the conference, an Indian pastor leaned over to me and pointed out the three leading pastors in that city of nine million people and said, "Those three pastors have never worked together, and only two of them rarely." After three days of hot, dusty meetings, the pastors extended the last meeting three hours after we had departed to the airport. I was overwhelmed by what the Lord did, but I didn't yet understand that is was the beginning of my call to the nations. As a youth I had always been fascinated when missionaries came to speak at my church, but I still was not making the full connection between that and my calling—yet God was shifting my identity bit by bit.

King David's unusual success stemmed from his commitment to navigate the challenges of change. He was passionate to pursue his call while remaining faithful in each season.

The shifts I am describing in this book show the unveiling and maturing of the unique deposit that Father God has placed into each of us. Each shift in our lives requires our personal discovery, maturing growth, testing, and finally our agreement with God and active obedience—to allow Him to use our lives for His purpose and glory.

Each of us must face several major shifts that life requires. Many of us will never venture far beyond the safety of those experiences. If our identity is defined by our assignment instead of who we are to Father God, the shift into our next season will be very difficult. Our activity has morphed from an assignment into our identity. Even though assignments can reveal identity, they can't be the source of our identity. Security in who we are gives us the strength and flexibility to take necessary risks in strategic moments.

If we have no hidden agenda, God can hide His agenda in us. God will anoint us to shift our identity and expectation, but He will not continually anoint us to prove who we are. He is anointing His servants to prove who He is. We must be awakened to who we are to Him and enter into that purpose. Our identity must embrace our destiny with obedient responses.

Every life shift is built upon our response to a challenge at the end of an old season or the very first step into the new season. Most often they are the same. The last step in the old season is also the first step into a new season. Make a timeline of your life and review the key events. Include both the uplifting and the devastating things. What did God build in you through those events? Strength is revealed and forged in difficult situations. Ask yourself, "What did I learn in those situations? What did it change in me?"

Whenever Jesus is moving in your life, the devil is about ten feet away looking for a way to block the opportunity that God is presenting to you. God isn't afraid to take on the enemy head-on. God planted the tree of life and the tree of the knowledge of good and evil next to each other. God presents Himself to mankind—within the sphere of the enemy's influence—with total confidence and calculated purpose. Our life of praise and obedience to God will defeat the enemy, who would neither praise Him nor obey Him.

God is supremely confident—He knows He is God and He always wins! He has never entertained losing for one second. He is also planning on winning through us! If we lose our focus of Him, we could suffer a loss. However, He never loses focus of our lives, even if we do. He paid too great a price to obtain us. He is always willing to clean, restore, and add something new to us. He is more willing than we are. Look at the cross one more time—He is committed to you.

David's identity was rooted in his relationship as a son unto Father God. This was the core factor of David's success. Identity shifts are more difficult than most people realize. If your core identity as a son isn't established, it's impossible to enter the fullness of each season in your destiny journey, even though you may succeed in the task at hand. King Saul never lost a battle until his last one, but he also didn't experience the fullness of his destiny.

Samuel the prophet decreed that David would be the next king of Israel when David was still a young boy. David fully received it and believed it when he heard it. However, it wasn't yet developed in David's identity, but was resting in his faith. The seed had taken root in faith, but the fruit of that seed was years away, with many roots and branches yet to be added.

It was easier for David to defeat Goliath than it was to take the throne of Israel. Defeating Goliath required faith, but taking the throne as king of Israel required identity. Faith focuses on God and His ability. Identity focuses on us and our ability. *It's easier to believe what God can do than to believe what He can do through us.* God is looking for people who believe that He can do it through them. Faith can peak in a moment, but identity requires a sustained vision. Identity must be held in place by thoughts we receive from Father God. Faith is more fruitful when it operates from our true identity.

Most believers are more comfortable focusing on God—yet God is very purposeful and comfortable focusing on us. In the scriptures, we often see God addressing people as He sees them and in reference to His calling on their lives. Then He reveals His identity and His desires that are connected to what He is about to do through them. God has built godly desires into your identity to empower your decisions to pursue your destiny.

When we are called, He always tells us who we are. It is absolutely necessary! When God visited Moses at the burning bush, God had to change the way Moses saw himself more than the way Moses saw God. Bringing an identity shift to his servants is probably one of God's most difficult jobs because it requires our agreement. Nonetheless, He can handle it! He has an awesome record taking the least expected to the greatest success! If, like Gideon, we will go in the strength we have, we will experience the strength He has.

The most powerful title granted to Jesus was Son of God. From the security of that identity, He became a servant of Father God. Jesus is the greatest servant who has ever lived because He had the greatest revelation that He was the Son whom the Father loved dearly. An orphan can't risk being a true servant. A true servant is not above or beneath those they are assisting. They are motivated by love to serve the Father, and it results in serving others with love. His love is the heart-beat of every true servant of God. God's love is required to complete obedience. Jesus served *from* the Father's pleasure and love, not to *obtain* it. Yet, He lived to please the Father, not Himself. Jesus exalted His Father and the Father exalted Him.

Identity flows from how we see ourselves. This is largely influenced by the opinions of others and the beliefs we draw from our conclusions of our life events. Our conclusions are a major hurdle for God to shift. Our view of the past creates our identity for the future. I grew up with two sisters. One was a year older, and one was a year younger, but both were much taller than I was. My father nicknamed me "Shrimp." It wasn't hurtful to me, but it wasn't helpful either. Once I over-heard my father telling others how proud he was of me, and that was a boost to my self-worth—but he would never tell me. It hijacked some of my confidence, but it also challenged me to find my worth in Father God. However, from the age of sixteen to nineteen, I grew almost eight inches and gained fifty pounds. When I returned from college, my youngest brother was astounded at my growth. Some of you have not yet hit your growth spurt!

We have a heavenly Father who openly demonstrated His love for us. He is knocking at the door of our hearts to talk with us. Our view must be formed from how He sees us. We must believe Him beyond our present assessment of ourselves. As we continue to behold His face, our identity is revealed. *He is our identity mirror.* How we see Him is directly connected to how we see ourselves. When we see Him in a greater light and in more truth, it shifts how we see ourselves as well. If we don't allow God to shift our identity in each new season, we will not reach our full destiny.

Complaining is often a telltale sign that we haven't yet shifted our identity to enter the new season. Complaining reveals that we see our circumstances as greater than our identity. Complaining may result in us dying in the wilderness between Egypt and the Promised Land. The Israelites couldn't shift their identity from slaves to warriors without coming into a deeper encounter with the Father. God desired it, but they refused. They saw with their own eyes the miracles that produced deliverance from Egypt, but it didn't shift their identity.

They chose a slave relationship over a "son relationship" with God. They were comfortable with the lifestyle of Egypt. They told Moses, "We are afraid of God. You go to Him and come back and tell us what He tells you" (Exod. 20:18–21, paraphrased). Because Israel saw God like Pharaoh, they related to Him the same way—as slaves. The slave masters would go to Pharaoh and come back and tell the Israelites what to do. Now they wanted Moses to play the same role. They wanted a position and a job—not a relationship.

If you lose your identity in Egypt, you cannot overcome the giants that are living in your promised land. Then the wilderness will become your future, not the place of transition. Joshua and Caleb kept their identity as sons while working as slaves in Egypt, and it gave them a perspective of victory when they saw the giants. They not only survived Egypt and the forty years in the wilderness, but they were also a source of courage, vision, and strength as they led the next generation into the Promised Land.

Your identity flows from your Father God to you, His son. What you have been saved from is not as great as what you have been saved for. God was focused on His people dwelling in the land He promised Abraham—but deliverance from Egypt was required to get them there! They were not ready for their new address.

This all sounds easier than it is. When you buy a new house, it doesn't feel like yours because it wasn't the day before. You have to live there for a while before it feels like it's yours. Often, it seems as if you are living in someone else's house for the first several months. You might even find yourself unconsciously driving back to your old house out of habit. The new house is legally and logically yours. But it isn't "yours" in your heart. Over time, as you paint, decorate and arrange the furniture, it feels more like your own. You may not be able to mark the exact moment, but you know when you "own" it. The Father needs you to "own" your destiny.

The more familiar you become with the house—the more it's yours. If it costs substantially more than your previous house, there can even be an underlying sense of discomfort in the midst of the excitement. If you aren't comfortable with the new level of authority and responsibility that accompanies your new season, you won't live in it confidently, which affects your proficiency. If you do not rest in your new dwelling place in the necessary time period, you will return to living at the lower level of the last season until the next window of opportunity arises or you simply step up.

Exciting new experiences are created when fresh faith flows through our new identity. Old gasoline may ruin a new car's engine. Likewise, fresh gasoline could start an old car, but it wouldn't be wise to take the old car on a long trip. Old cars are fun to look at and talk about, but they aren't intended for everyday use or for long trips. They will not be fun in either application. I have lived long enough to see teenagers with old identities suffer from loss of purpose and vision. I have also seen retirees with new identities who are zealous and passionate for life. God is the Rock of Ages. He needs to be your rock in each of your "ages."

Living from—and for—yourself will produce pride or fear. Both are self-based, not Father-based! Living in the Father and listening to Him gives you a correct self-assessment. If you receive what the Father speaks to your heart, you can step into a new season. Your successful journey is based on a heart that continues to listen for His voice.

Our agreement with truth is required for both faith and identity. Identity is more difficult to grasp because we approach it incorrectly. Traditionally in our culture, we gain our identity from what we do, instead of who we are. However, if you are a relative of John Kennedy or George Bush, your identity as a politician and leader is already established because of your father's success. Our identity flows from our Father— naturally and spiritually. Our Father God is very successful in every arena of life that He created for His sons.

God will give us watershed events with unusual results to invite us into an identity shift. He knows how we think apart from a mature relationship with Him. He will meet us where we live and think in order to take us to where He lives and thinks.

God gives us different experiences to create different thoughts to form a different identity. We must then live from Him in our new identity, not from the experiences. *A new way of thinking cannot be contained in an old identity.* The old identity will eventually derail the new set of thoughts generated by a new experience if we do not allow those thoughts to shift our identity.

It is essential to live from our new identity in order to maintain the elevated season we have just entered. *Our new season is marked with assignments that were not granted to us in the past, even though they were promised.* He reveals dreams of the future to shift us and our path. Pursuing our destiny requires more of Him by design and purpose. He is the One who is building identity in us.

A collage of new thoughts creates a new process of reasoning and conclusions that allows us to embark upon new assignments. Possibility thinking and problem solving are now functioning at a new level that empowers us to shift the earth. Until heaven shifts us, we cannot shift the earth. What we gain in identity shifts the way we evaluate situations. Until we think differently, nothing new will flow from our life. One new thought can elevate what we already know to a superior level.

Jesus operated from His primary identity as the Son of God, and it empowered Him to shift things on the earth. More importantly, Jesus shifted the activity of twelve men and the identity of eleven. Judas shifted his activity as he walked with Jesus. He saw the power of God work through him, but he never entered into a relationship with Jesus. Judas never became a son; rather, he remained an orphan. He became a thief and then a betrayer. Out of his broken identity he fulfilled an assignment he could not bear.

At the Last Supper, Jesus plainly said that one of them would betray Him, but none of the disciples knew who it was.

They had been together three years. How could this be? They reflected on the activity of each disciple, but only Jesus knew the identity of each one of them. They may have suspected Peter, since they heard Jesus tell him, "Get behind Me, Satan!" But Jesus revealed Peter's identity as a "rock" prior to that remark. His identity as a "rock" propelled Peter beyond his denial of Jesus to the day of Pentecost. Jesus knew Peter's assignment for that day was rooted in his identity that Jesus revealed. So is ours. Jesus declared Peter's identity before He established it in him. *He speaks our identity—then He builds it in us.*

Jesus is speaking our identity—we must believe it so He can build it in us. That is the important first step. Now we must guard that identity through the storms of life. The Bride of Christ is stepping up into Him and discovering herself in the process. She will walk in Jesus on this earth. There is a glory Jesus has prayed for us to receive so that we could experience an identity shift.

Our assignments with Him are shifting the earth with a force that has never been witnessed in any age. It has been the same strategy in the past with Abraham, Moses, Esther, David, Elijah, and the faithful disciples of Jesus—and it is increasing.

Dreams do not hinge on our natural abilities. *Dreams that shift the earth hinge on identity.* God dreams shift the identity of the dreamer. The unique thoughts that accompany those dreams create a new paradigm. A paradigm is a model or pattern for something that may be copied or followed. It is a theory or a group of ideas about how something should be. God made each person with the capacity to dream. Dreaming comes more naturally than thinking—we can dream while we are asleep.

Can we live in that new identity, or are we just making occasional visits? New vision and increased authority are given to us by God so that we can address greater needs and more difficult issues in His kingdom. Our new identity is not to give us an easier life, but rather a more fruitful one. When God desires to accomplish new tasks through you, it requires an identity shift and a new level of faith. These shifts are initiated through desires God has put in us, or through things that He causes to disturb us.

If we don't see ourselves as God sees us, we cannot agree to His assignment. God had to talk Moses into what He was showing him, because Moses did not see himself as God did. When God turned the staff in Moses's hand into a snake, it gave him faith that he had entered a promised season. The staff spoke of the new authority released to Moses to accomplish his assignment in Egypt. Little did he know that it would be a key for crossing the Red Sea, bringing water out of a rock, and the determiner of victory for the armies that followed Joshua into battle. Moses's own staff became God's rod—in the hands of Moses. When He changes what we carry, it will change us and our activities forever.

When God reveals our future, it also reveals our new identity in "seed form," which must be planted and watered. Visions from Him are delayed or lost if there isn't an identity shift or an "activity shift." When we shift our activity, it affects our identity. This is an act of faith based on obedience to the vision and His instructions. It pleases God when we respond in faith with action. He will give us victories to change our mindsets.

Moses' identity shifted dramatically when he stood in front of Pharaoh in the palace. He was no longer an Egyptian leader or a hunted fugitive—he was the deliverer of Israel. When Israel was trapped by Egypt's army at the Red Sea, Moses was on a different assignment, one requiring a different part of his identity—that of military leader. Yet another aspect of his identity as an intercessor was revealed on the mountain of glory as he entered the second time. As he carried the Ten Commandments down the mountain, it may not have yet occurred to him that he was about to be the judge of Israel. There are multi-faceted dimensions of our identity that will be developed as we follow the Lord, and being a son is the foundation of them all.

David entered the battle as a shepherd boy, but he left it as a warrior. God shifted David's identity in an incredible way through that great victory. David was never again seen as a shepherd boy by anyone in Israel. He was not only seen as a warrior, but also a leader in the armies of Israel.

David's leadership was established as he stepped forward to face Goliath in battle.

Everything must be established in the mouth of two or three witnesses. These witnesses are several events with the verbalized consensus of others. David defeated Goliath, protected the city of Keilah from the Philistines and recovered all after the great loss at Ziklag. If others see our identity shift through new activity in our lives and then we agree with their observation, our identity is established. If we do not receive our new identity, eventually they will agree with us.

Our experience becomes an event we will talk about, but it is not the "game changer" to our identity as God intended. We might be upset with those who seemingly are keeping us from our new season—yet they simply agreed with us. God experiences create momentum and a window of opportunity that we must apprehend. However, we can normally recapture the window to our new season as we agree with God and respond to His assignments to us.

It's critical that we understand what God is doing in us while He is moving through us. If we can perceive and receive our new identity, we will be able to step into our new season with greater ease as we operate in our new identity and expand its boundaries.

Everything must be established in the mouth of two or three witnesses. When two or three people of influence and maturity are saying the same things about our new identity, it will establish a new base of authority, connected to our purpose, to thrive in our new season. We may see it before or after they do, but we must agree to move forward.

My older sister was a straight-A student. When I came to my first history class in seventh grade, my new teacher Mr. Carl Hill smiled and spoke loud enough for all to hear, "Another Mast!" After seeing my results on his first surprise quiz, he handed me my paper and announced with a tone of disapproval, "You're not your sister." To me, it meant that I wasn't a good student. The subtle reasoning that followed was a strike against my destiny. If I wasn't a good student, how could I ever be a good teacher?

When I became a pastor, that experience worked against me because of the hidden judgment that I had formed against myself. After a very good meeting in another church, I remarked to the pastor that I really enjoyed the meeting, but that I wished I were a better teacher. Pastor Rob Meyer said, "Dale, you are one of the best teachers I know. Your teachings are always so interesting." My judgment against myself was breaking. It actually changed my attitude and the way I studied the scriptures and taught.

A short time later, the very same Carl Hill invited me to speak at the men's group in his church. After I was done, Carl complemented me on the teaching and told me that he had heard so many good things about me—he just had to have me come and speak to his group. It had been over twenty years since I had sat in his history class. Looking back now, I see that I didn't clearly understand that God was addressing a specific event in my life.

God also addressed this issue of intelligence again ten years later. I had just finished teaching an afternoon session for Arise 5, a network of churches headquartered in Japan. Ron Sawka, the leader of Arise 5, and I were discussing some of the points I had just finished teaching. He paused, looked at me, and asked, "Are you a genius?" It struck me as odd when he said it, but God used that question to unravel the last vestiges of "You're not your sister." I didn't answer yes or no. Rather, I simply let his question minister life to me. The last of the negative thoughts were being removed, and the positive mindset was being completed.

As I was finishing writing this book, I hit a real wall of discouragement. Pastor Dave Hess sent me an email that very day remarking how much he'd enjoyed the rough draft. Then, the Lord reminded me that He sent Carl back into my life to get over this "hill" of inferiority. God knew where it started, and he was bringing it to an end. Our Father God is so wonderful and yet very practical. He also reminded me that I had become one of Carl Hill's favorite students and had made As in his class. Why is it we remember the negative so quickly and the positive so briefly? What thoughts of inferiority has the enemy placed in your mind to disrupt your destiny? What subtle negative reasoning is blocking you from reaching your destiny? Our Father God is coming into your life to break those thoughts of inferiority and to expose hidden judgments.

Defeating Goliath marked the beginning of a new season in David's life. When David defeated him, the armies of Israel engaged in battle. David wasn't planning to lead the army of Israel into a victorious battle when he first saw Goliath, but God already had a plan for David. David stepped up into his new level of vision while standing before Goliath. He saw more at that place than he did while presenting himself to King Saul before the battle. He decreed his victory to Goliath before he hurled the first stone. Our victories should inspire others to victory. If we are the only one who wins, it isn't God's best. David became a leader in the eyes of the warriors. God turns difficult challenges into victories in our life to shift our identity. ***It takes a Goliath to reveal a David!***

The Quest for Significance

Deep in the heart of every person, God has placed *a desire for significance*. That desire can be traded for survival after a heart-crushing experience. Lurking beneath the ashes of heartache is a dream that still whispers to your heart.

People throw their hands up and proclaim that they couldn't care less as they try to ease the pain inside. That proclamation reveals how much they cared before their dream was crushed. We can lose our ability to dream. Have we chosen not to dream anymore? Has our faith been silenced by events we cannot explain? If we have the answer to everything, we will never need faith. Faith is birthed in God and is not dependent upon having an answer for every undesirable event in our life.

In my second year of pastoring, there was a terrible split that occurred with one of my close leaders. Over the next fifteen years the relationship improved, but there were still several unresolved issues. Trying to understand the last of those details, I brought it before the Lord. He answered me so clearly: "If you try to figure it out, you are going to come up with the wrong answer and it will hurt you. I am not going to tell you any more. Can you trust Me?" I realized that I could trust Him without the answer. The answer is not peace—*He is peace*. Trust is not based on explanations—it is based on relationship. Over the following decade, God brought total healing to that relationship without ever giving me the answer to the question I felt was so vital. Even the desire to have those answers went away.

Many Christians want Goliath testimonies while fighting munchkins. Do we really want greater miracles? Then we must face greater problems that we can do nothing about in the natural. I am talking about huge problems that have the ability to destroy us! Do you still want greater miracles? Many want a miracle-filled life without horrendous problems. That is impossible by definition!

David perceived that God had established him as king for the sake of Israel—not for the sake of his ministry. Whatever God establishes in us is directly connected to what we will do to help others. Jesus didn't leave heaven to help Himself, but to help us. He represented and honored Father God to the earth.

God will place many of these greater difficulties in front of us, but He wants us to confront these situations by choice. David aggressively chased the lion down to save a lamb. He did not avoid problems—he pursued them. David couldn't believe that the army of Israel was allowing that uncircumcised Philistine to taunt the armies of the living God.

David chose to take on Goliath because he believed that God would make him king someday. David's vision of his future fueled his faith for his present battle. If Samuel prophesied that he would be the king of Israel, how could he possibly die in this battle? Goliath was actually a huge stepping stone to David's "God dream." Your defeated "Goliaths" release heaven's promotions. Of course, it helps to have first killed a lion and a bear before running toward Goliath. David was showing up—not showing off.

Great leaders have always risen from trying times. One of the most horrific periods of American history, the Civil War, forged one of our greatest presidents, Abraham Lincoln. As the meaning of his biblical name foreshadowed, he would be the "father of many nations" within one nation—to bring them into unity. Fathers are most needed in difficult times. If it hadn't been for the Civil War and his ability to bring the nation together as one, it is doubtful that Abraham Lincoln would be regarded today as one of the greatest and most respected presidents. This wasn't true in his day, but history clarifies the greatness of a man who stands for the ageless principles of truth—and not for the momentary convenience of compromise.

Your identity and character are dramatically revealed in the worst of times. It takes a crisis to reveal a hero. Convictions and character are developed over the years, even though their decisive actions were determined in moments.

David, the Forgotten Son

"So he asked Jesse, 'Are these all the sons you have?' 'There is still the youngest,' Jesse answered. 'He is tending the sheep.' Samuel said, 'Send for him; we will not sit down until he arrives'" (1 Sam. 16:11, NIV).

When Samuel came to Jesse's house looking to anoint a king, David was forgotten. Some Bible scholars believe that David was actually not a son from Jesse's wife, but rather a son born to him out of an affair with one of the handmaidens. David states that "in sin my mother conceived me" (Ps. 51:5). Some believe this statement points to the nature of David's birth rather than the overall state of mankind. The above verse that says David was Jesse's "youngest" could also mean a "no-account" son. This would indicate that David wouldn't have any inheritance. In Jewish culture, it would suggest that he wasn't a legitimate heir. This may be why Jesse never called David to stand with the rest of his sons in front of Samuel.

If David was Jesse's favorite, he would have called him first and would have chosen David to stand at the front of the line beside him as the other brothers found their place. David was chosen by the prophet over his brothers in their presence. That was an awkward situation with little celebration by David or his brothers. When God promotes you among those who desired your promotion, you must receive it humbly with faith and joy—quietly. David spoke nothing to his father or brothers at that time, but he treasured this event in his heart.

In this regard, David had maturity and wisdom that Joseph had to learn the hard way. Joseph shared his dreams with his brothers without realizing how it stirred up the rejection they already felt from their father. Joseph's brothers thought that they would never have a place in their father's heart unless Joseph was removed. When Joseph shared his dream that even his father and mother, along with all his brothers, would bow down to him, his father rebuked him. It is not appropriate to share all of your dreams with everyone. In Joseph's case, it worked for his good and proved truths that could not have been established in scriptures without the rejection of his brothers—but David's example is a better one to model.

David was overlooked by his own father—this isn't a trivial issue. Comparison among siblings is one of the most damaging activities in normal dysfunctional families of which we're all a part. Children naturally evaluate themselves in comparative situations, even before factoring in the degrading comments of others. Parents naturally want their children to fulfill goals that they never did. When they start living their dreams through their children, it becomes very dangerous. We are to live our dreams through Christ.

At a family Christmas gathering with my siblings—six of us in all—I asked them who they thought had it the easiest or was the most spoiled by our parents as we grew up. Our ages ranged from forty to sixty, so we had many years to reflect on our childhood. There were three or four opinions with excellent points, but no one thought they had it the easiest! That fact alone amazed me. Also, no one disagreed with the points that were made about them—yet they didn't believe that made them the most favored. Maybe the other siblings thought they would have experienced more love if those things would have happened for them. Each sibling's view had truth based on personal experiences, but none of us could totally comprehend the other sibling's life. It is important to try to understand, but caring about the person is the greatest connection.

In our family there was a space of nine years between the two groups of three siblings. As each group recounted their childhoods, we realized that our parents had matured over those nine years. The older ones all agreed on shared experiences, as did the younger set—but the older and the younger sets of experiences did not reflect each other. It was an insightful event that shifted my view of our family dynamics and the life of each of my siblings.

"When they measure themselves by themselves and compare themselves with themselves, they are not wise" (2 Cor. 10:12).

The stronghold of comparison established in childhood grows during our school years. Then, our career becomes the next hotbed for comparisons. Perception and family dynamics set life's pattern of proving worth and identity. Insecurity coupled with performance clouds the relationship that God and others desire to have with us. It hampers the healthy development of our identity. Insecurity drives performance, but it always steals contentment in the midst of accomplishments.

Insecurity always wonders if it was good enough. Until we see ourselves and our life through Father God's eyes of love, there will not be the needed security that releases true authority to accomplish and maintain our destiny. Most of us are better *doers* than *be-ers*. The great "I Am" is also calling us to be *i-am-ers* too! True *i-am-ers* do the will of God from His presence and pleasure with great peace and power! Look at the creative works of the great "I Am!" We must believe that He wants to do something creative through us.

Prayer: Holy Spirit, reveal to me any event from the past that birthed insecurity in me. I forgive them and myself. I break the spirit of shame that entered my life through that event. Lord, remove any false identity I received from it. I receive from You, Father, the double honor You promised me in Your Word. Renew my mind to agree with You, Father God. Reveal to me any time I slipped back into performance, insecurity, and that false identity. I choose to abide in the honor that You have placed on my life.

In the Shadow of Eliab

Eliab was an impressive man. He was an obvious choice to Jesse, and even to Samuel, who was one of the most accurate prophets in history! God planted Eliab next to David for David's own good. God will place others with obvious talents and greatness beside us, forcing us to deal with our own insecurities. Every David must grow up in the shadow of an Eliab. David had to live in the shadow of Eliab while focusing on the presence of God. Your Heavenly Father will never allow you to step into your identity via the circus of comparison. His sons are established in the Father's throne room. As we are seated next to our Father God in heavenly places, our identity is revealed. We must pray from the seat of honor like Jesus—not the church pew.

Eliab was not David's problem, but rather a challenge to his focus. Determining his value in Eliab's shadow would simply have been the result of David's own internalized comparisons to him, which would have resulted in self-rejection or pride. True greatness will never emerge until we are comfortable in our own skin. When we compare ourselves to others, we will be deceived. Rejoicing and receiving who

God has made us is a form of worship. Lucifer wasn't content with his identity or assignments. Don't fall into his trap. Son, find your identity in the shadow of your Almighty Father.

An eagle looks majestic as it soars across the sky. Everyone admires eagles—far more than chickens. But without chickens, there wouldn't be eggs for breakfast or meat for the hundreds of wonderful chicken dishes eaten around the world! Furthermore, eagles lay only two eggs a year, whereas a chicken lays as many as two hundred and sixty! The chicken is an "eagle" egg layer, and the eagle is a "chicken" egg layer! They both are birds created by the Father for very different purposes. Keep with your purpose! If the eagle and the chicken were to compare themselves to each other, it would produce pride or insecurity. Insecurity always focuses on what we can't do. The chicken must refuse to live in the shadow of the eagle. Insecurity is a *binding* force, and pride is a *blinding* force. Confidence, however, is a liberating force that empowers us for our destiny.

Many of us have used a knife as a screwdriver. It can work in a pinch, but that's not its purpose. Sometimes the tip of the knife breaks, or the screw becomes deformed as the screw refuses to budge. Nothing is as effective for that screw as the correct screwdriver. Everything created has a purpose. It is most effective when used for that specific purpose. Some tools only have one purpose, and they make a seemingly impossible task simple and easy. Sometimes we must take care of things that are not our greatest purpose.

That is a time to judge our faithfulness—not our abilities compared to those who are gifted in that specific area. The greatest anointing on our life will occur when we enter into our purpose.

No one can ever steal our place or position of destiny. They might jump in ahead of us and seemingly push us backwards. However, that is an event—not the story. Our reaction to that event is a greater factor than what they did. God will allow people to jump in front of us to make sure we are pursuing Him and not just our future. We must refuse to jump into a race of desperation or walk away from our call in frustration. Keep at it! We run our race before the Father. Our walk with God is our race. He will take care of our destiny if we keep our heart pure following His path and His directions. Purity without direction is holy ineffectiveness. Direction without purity is carnal activity. Purity and direction release the plans, the power, and the purposes of God.

False humility will cripple us from taking our place of authority and blessing in due season. False humility carries a fragrance of unworthiness—with an underlying odor of pride. False humility avoids responsibility and assignments from heaven, because of the fear of criticism and failure. False humility focuses on the wrongs we have not committed in a certain area of life, but others did as they helped many. It deceives us into believing that we are more spiritual. We may not have done the wrongs they did, but actually we have done nothing in that particular area of life to honor God. Obedience to God will keep false humility from ruining our lives. True humility realizes how God is using us in a powerful way in spite of our imperfections because we are committed to Him and to pursuing His will.

God can shift our lives in a day, but it will take a journey to arrive at that day. Jesus lived thirty years before He stepped into His ministry for three years—and He changed the world. Can we believe there are three good years still ahead of us? We can't waste our lives on regret. We must live the days He has given us. We should be passionate, purposeful, persistent, and patient as we move toward our destiny with great expectations.

"When they arrived, Samuel saw Eliab and thought, 'Surely the Lord's anointed stands here before the Lord.' But the Lord said to Samuel, 'Do not consider his appearance or his height, for I have rejected him. The Lord does not look at the things people look at. People look at the outward appearance, but the Lord looks at the heart'" (1 Sam. 16:6–7, NIV).

Eliab was favored by all and he knew it. He was the prophet's first pick. Samuel was moved by the looks of this impressive young man. Physically, Eliab was similar to Saul. Both were tall, handsome men. Samuel was stuck in a "Saul" search mode. Do you remember how outstanding Saul was? In 1 Samuel 9:2, we read that "Kish had a choice and handsome son whose name was Saul. There was not a more handsome person than he among the children of Israel. From his shoulders upward he was taller than any of the people."

Similarly, Eliab was striking in appearance. He was an outstanding warrior of impressive size. Eliab watched the approving smile on Samuel's face turn into a blank stare as God corrected His prophet. Eliab went from "surely accepted" to "absolutely rejected" as God spoke to Samuel.

Consider the following verse: "Thus Samuel grew and the Lord was with him and let none of his words fail" (1 Sam. 3:19, NASB). We must understand that not all of Samuel's thoughts were from God, but Samuel kept listening until he heard what God said. Samuel didn't speak too quickly as Nathan did when he told David to build God's house; rather, he waited until God spoke to him. Therefore, his words didn't "fall to the ground" (3:19, NKJV). Experience and maturity can be a trap if we don't listen or inquire of God when we are certain what we should do.

"Jesse had seven of his sons pass before Samuel, but Samuel said to him, 'The Lord has not chosen these.' So he asked Jesse, 'Are these all the sons you have?'" (1 Sam. 16:10–11, NIV). I'm confident Jesse didn't forget he had a son named David, but he must have been sure that Samuel was going to choose Eliab. Jesse was stunned. Maybe he was expecting Samuel to come back to Eliab and chose him after examining the others. Jesse didn't even consider David a remote possibility.

Our earthly father's opinion of us isn't our limitation. Many struggle to rise above the words of their fathers. Hearing the words of Father God and "fathers" in the Spirit is the only way to break through what our natural father may have said. What our father never said that would have brought value to our identity could be an even greater loss.

David was Israel's greatest king. Jesus will sit upon the throne of David—not Abraham's or Elijah's throne, yet Jesse didn't perceive it. We may well have to live beyond our father's opinion of our life. Father God was dreaming of our purpose when He created us. He has greater dreams for our lives than we could ever imagine.

Chapter Two

ANOINTED BY GREATNESS

D avid's life was profoundly impacted when he was anointed by Samuel in several dimensions. The words of Samuel confirmed David as the next king of Israel—creating an identity, a dream and a new mindset. Samuel anointed David with oil and released the power of the Holy Spirit to rest on him—authority. Yet Samuel poured more than oil over David's life—he poured his greatness into David.

Samuel was not only the prophet of Israel, but he was also like the president. He was the military leader that led them into war as the military leader, before Saul was made king. He was the judge of the entire nation. He was also the spiritual leader of Israel. It was an unexpected visit from a very powerful man. He literally came out of retirement for this event. That's why the town shook with fear when he arrived.

First and foremost, greatness was spoken over David's life by the *greatest* prophet alive. Samuel was a legend. The greatness that Samuel had achieved qualified him to give underrated

David a vision and impartation for his future. He didn't just pour the anointing oil over David's head—he also poured his greatness over David's identity. It's not just what is done that has impact, but also who does it. God could have used another prophet to speak over David, but God used Samuel's greatness to impact David's identity. David needed more than a word from God; he needed his value and identity elevated in order to fulfill the words Samuel spoke over him.

Many people could tell us that we will become a great evangelist, but if Billy Graham, one of the greatest evangelists, met with us at God's request, it would have a much greater impact. Greatness is a part of Father God's nature that He pours over His sons so that He can work through them and they can work with Him. Once we are established in greatness, whom will we pour it over? Be listening to heaven; a "David" could be passing in front of you now.

A sudden scheduling conflict brought Bishop Bill Hamon to our church for a series of meetings. He told us that he felt the true reason he came was not for the meetings, but to ordain LuAnne and me. I realized that he had mentored me in the prophetic gift that God had given me. LuAnne mentioned that he was such a father to her. In the natural, you do not choose your father; rather, you simply recognize who birthed you. Around the world, Bishop Hamon is recognized as a leading father of the prophetic movement. He is our spiritual covering. In the last three years, Bishop and Mom Hamon spoke at our church and spent time with us. They spoke to our destiny, and impacted our identity with their greatness.

Bishop Anne Gimenez invited us to pray at "America For Jesus (AFJ)." John Gimenez and she orchestrated the greatest national prayer meetings of our generation at three different "Washington For Jesus" gatherings. The first gathering, back in 1980, numbered over 700,000. More recently, Bishop Anne was gathering leaders from around the nation to pray for America in Philadelphia. I had been the prayer coordinator for Delaware for many years, but this was my first national event.

Lou Engle led our group in prayer along with Rick Joyner, Wesley and Stacey Campbell and many others at AFJ. Lou Engle called my name and told me that it was my assignment to take down the spirit of Jezebel. It was a new assignment with a new level of authority released to my wife and me. We have always prayed for the nations as we minister abroad, but this assignment released a new honor and increased our realm of authority.

Over a year later, Bishop Anne invited me to be a part of the ceremony to install John and Robin Blanchard as pastors at The Rock Church. As I was sitting on the stage with Pat Robertson of the 700 Club, Billy Wilson, president of ORU, Paul Johansson, president of Elim Bible Institute, and David Minor, a great prophet who touched many ministries — something very special was released into the depths of my heart. As the event started, I had a deep, quiet moment between me and Father God.

I experienced something like David did. I felt like clay, and the glory of God was forming my identity on the potter's wheel. He is the glory and the lifter of our head. These events of honor are designed by Father God to mold us for His future purpose. These are important moments that God orchestrates in our lives to let us see our value to Him in a different light. Bishop Anne honored me in a very impactful way. We must understand what the Father has shifted so that we can access that part of our destiny in a new way and in a greater level.

David moved quickly toward his destiny because his identity was rooted in Father God. The enemy tries to destroy our relationship with our natural father so that he can dominate our relationship with our heavenly father. The enemy will use our natural father's anger or emotional distance to blind us from seeing what we are called to enjoy with our heavenly Father. From childhood, David had to live beyond the opinion of his father and brothers. God helped him by sending great men his way to establish his value at a young age.

New Honor, New Season

God will bring new people into our lives to shift our identity with new honor. They will open doors for us that we could not access by ourselves, and they will give us honor among those who have greater honor. It will release a new flow of activity, favor, and finances beyond that which we have ever known. These people will cause us to see ourselves in a new light. New recognition and respect causes our identity to mature. Living in that new honor is the key to our destiny. It generates a greater anointing to accomplish a greater purpose. Honor flows from our reputation of integrity and it creates new privileges

Greater vision emerges from new honor. If we walk in the light of honor, we will bear much fruit. Living in honor is a walk in our Father's deep love—loving Him and those around us. Honor is harder to maintain than most understand. Bragging is a desperate attempt to create it—arguing is a fearful way of keeping it—and hiding is shame's way of avoiding it.

Honor is an anointed force that accelerates the kingdom of God and its activities on the earth. When Jehoshaphat and the people honored the Lord in worship, the enemy was defeated as the Lord fought the battle! Jesus—heaven's best— could do no miracles in his hometown because of a lack of honor (Mark 6:4). Esther used the honor she received from King Xerxes to save the Jews from Haman's evil plot.

Honor creates identity shifts and opens new spheres of authority. The enemy also knows that dishonor restricts the identity and authority we will need to fulfill God's amazing plan for our lives that will help so many others. He can't cancel the plans of heaven, so he creates events specifically intended to dishonor us. When we look at the negative events in our lives, we need to see beyond the person and the event— discerning the hand of the enemy. If we keep giving honor to the Lord and to others, we will receive it from the Lord and from others—and the enemy cannot stop us. It is also very important to realize that some people are not safe to have a trusted place in your life. David honored and served King Saul, but he realized that he couldn't trust him.

We must understand the principles of honor, but more importantly, we're learning how to receive and give it. Jesus openly received honor from the Father and gave it back to Him. It is the currency of heaven, but not of earth. Jealousy and insecurity are the assassins of honor. Without honor, every person will accomplish much less. Honor causes the activities of heaven to fill earth. The Holy Spirit moves when the Father is honored and worshiped. Honor brings out the best in everyone.

There are many others God used very naturally to impact my life and destiny. It started for me when I was very young. I remember Uncle Laban sitting on a couch holding his black hat in his hands looking at me when I was seven saying, "When you grow up, you ought to be a preacher." I don't know why he said it to me. He must have been observing me as I was playing. Another time, after I finished giving an answer to the teacher of the youth class, the pastor's daughter turned around, as I was sitting in the pew behind her, and declared, "You ought to be a pastor!" There are many things in life I can't remember, but those are events I will never forget!

As a baby, my grandfather was adopted into an Amish home. They had too many girls and needed another boy to work the farm. When he was eight, he came home crying after the other children told him he wasn't a part of the family. When he asked his mother if it was true, she kept on cooking and said "It's true." She never stopped to comfort him as he cried and stumbled toward his bedroom.

The orphan spirit was released over him, and it flowed to his children. There were occasional letters from a relative of his birth mother in Kansas that were sent to his wife. One of my uncles—at forty years old—traveled from Delaware to Kansas to meet his "birth" grandmother. He met a half-cousin playing baseball in the front yard who told him, "Your grandmother lives in that house. If you knock on the door, she'll answer and you can meet her. But as far as we are concerned, you don't exist. Don't ever come back here again." My uncle was trying to think of what to say to her as he raised his hand to knock on the door. He stood there for several minutes. He dropped his hand and then his head—then he walked away dejectedly. He struggled with the same depression that his own father faced.

Several years ago, my uncles decided it was time for one last attempt to discover their roots and meet their biological family if anyone was still alive. The journey seemed over at the gravesite of their "birth" grandmother, Ruth. No one in town knew anything about her family. My first cousin posted on an ancestry website asking if anyone knew Ruth Foyak. A woman responded who lived in Norman, Oklahoma, just four hours from Ruth's gravesite. She invited them to come for a meal. Uncle Willie called me to let me know and invited me to come. I knew that it was very important for me to be there, so LuAnne and I flew out.

My uncles and aunts were so excited to meet them—it seemed like a dream. The man who was our relative made us soup. His wife's hobby was studying ancestry. She also visited the libraries where her relatives had lived—tracing their lives through old newspaper archives to find out anything about them. She literally had three books of family history for the family who had no history. She said, "I can tell you anything about your family history you would like to know. The American Airlines Flight 93 crashed into a field owned by one of your relatives during the 9/11 attack. One of your great, great, great grandfathers was Phillip Marsteller, a close friend of President George Washington." Martha Washington specifically requested in writing that Col. Marsteller, who was not a Mason, be one of the President's pallbearers. Washington's pallbearers included six colonels— Philip being one of them—who had served under General Washington during the Revolutionary War. History and honor were returned to our family—which had neither.

We had shared with them the story and the hurt that had never been healed. I asked them if they would bless me with the family blessing that my grandfather Clarence Mast never received. He said that he would be more than happy to do it. As he was blessing me, he was pouring the greatness of my family heritage, which had never been released, over me. My uncles started weeping the tears of a child who was never wanted or blessed. They were all successful in careers, but this was the blessing of belonging and identity. As he released honor and celebrated our presence, it broke the orphan spirit over the Clarence Mast family. Our destiny flourishes in the blessing of inheritance.

Honor is a spiritual force that elevates identity and opens doors to destiny. As David played his harp before the king, he started experiencing the honor shift needed for his destiny. He was in an environment of honor—a palace—playing for the man God had greatly honored—King Saul. For strategic reasons, God brought David into the very place He had planned for his destiny. The dream was becoming more real. David was serving in a different role in the king's palace where he would eventually reign. While still a shepherd and minstrel, David was "rubbing shoulders" with the most important people in Israel. God was initiating David into a very different world that was directly connected to his call—with which he needed to become familiar. As David played his harp each day, he observed what a king did. Our days of training are critical for our success.

Saul never lost a battle except the last one in which he died. He was an elite warrior who was victorious over Israel's enemies. When David heard of Saul's death he said, "How the mighty have fallen!" (2 Sam. 1:19) He wasn't being generous—he was being truthful. Nonetheless, God rejected Saul after a great victory because of his lack of obedience.

Our ability to win the battle is not the mark of greatness in God's kingdom.

In the midst of a great victory, we can lose our relationship with Father God and still keep our position. We see the roots of rebellion, which is like witchcraft, surfacing in Saul's life. Saul wanted to be honored by Samuel in front of the people more than he desired to honor God by his obedience. Even when confronted by Samuel, Saul's lack of repentance is astounding. Rebellion is a toxic heart issue. His lack of repentance was a greater issue than the sin committed. Those roots of unrepentant rebellion literally drew Saul to a witch before he died in his last battle.

Jonathan was the king's son and heir to the throne. Like his father, he was also a great warrior. By stepping out in faith, he and his armor bearer facilitated a major victory over the Philistines (1 Sam. 14). Jonathan loved David. Their bond of friendship and David's marriage to the king's daughter placed him right in the middle of Israel's "first family." Remarkably, Jonathan knew and desired that David would be the next king of Israel! (1 Sam. 23:16–17) David built a relationship with Jonathan that was greater than the throne they could not share. Jonathan—the heir apparent to the throne of Israel—humbly and joyfully poured his greatness over David's life.

After David spared Saul's life the second time, Saul prophesied—in front of David's mighty men and Saul's three thousand best warriors—that David would be the next king of Israel.

> *"When David finished saying this, Saul asked, 'Is that*
> *your voice, David my son?' And he wept aloud. 'You*
> *are more righteous than I,' he said. ... 'I know that you*
> *will surely be king and that the kingdom of Israel will be*
> *established in your hands.'" (1 Sam. 24:16–17, 20, NIV)*

Simultaneously, God spoke David's greatness into the hearts of David's men and Saul's warriors through the mouth of Saul! These words would have been heard by Abner, who later brought Israel to David at Hebron. God will use your adversaries to convince you that you will make it. Saul was hunting David down when he lifted him up. In the middle of great opposition, the integrity of David's heart opened up the heavens for him to be exalted by his oppressor. Our godly response to criticism will create a turning point for our destiny.

The Lord had given me honor to be a regional leader in a network of churches. The man who was given administrative oversight of the entire network became a friend as we worked together over the next several years. He decided to launch a new program modeled from the business world that each regional leader would be required to facilitate in their churches. I could see the value of the program, but there was a component I simply did not see as scriptural or necessary. His attitude toward me became adversarial in a short period of time. The leader wasn't sure whether or not he wanted to use the administrator's program. I told my leader I'd willing resign if he decided go forward with the administrator's program—knowing it was not my decision nor could I commit to it with a clear conscience. A month later, the leader called me and said that he would take me up on my resignation, as the network was going forward with the program.

For a short season, I sat in the same meetings I used to lead. It was hurtful. But as I was leaving the regional meeting, I literally lifted both hands to the Lord and thanked Him for His goodness to me. I enjoyed a very deep time of worship for several hours as I drove home. The pain left. When I got home, I found a letter in the mailbox with an address I didn't recognize. The letter stated that I was nominated and accepted to be a part of the International Coalition of Apostles (ICA). I wonder what God will put in your mailbox when you turn your eyes toward Him, instead of toward the hurt. Our response to the hurt is more important than the event that caused it. Years later, I was told that it had been my leader, as well as Chuck Pierce, who had nominated me for acceptance into ICA. I honored my leader when I did not agree and he honored me. If we can give honor when we feel rejected, we will never be stopped.

Father God is anointing spiritual fathers who know how to pour their greatness over their sons and daughters. That greatness is poured out through love and words of encouragement. It is transferred through meaningful time spent together. The amount of time spent together is not as important as the depth of conversation. It takes a father to instill greatness in those who are unrecognized and undeveloped. Samuel was a father who poured his greatness over David's identity. Whom will we pour our greatness over?

God visited Samuel and asked him, "How long will you mourn for Saul? Fill your horn with oil and be on your way" (1 Sam. 16:1, NIV). Even God regretted making Saul king. Leaders, you will not do better than God, but keep on raising up leaders. Samuel's value to God was not determined by his own sons or by King Saul. There is a David in a field near you. He needs you to make it. He doesn't know he is the next King of Israel. David and Samuel never enjoyed a long-term friendship, yet Samuel's impact on David life was profound. There are those that you will pour your greatness over for a short time who will become greater than those whom you pour your life into every day. Samuel never lived to see David become king. The greatest fruit of your ministry may be viewed from heaven.

The Power of Celebration

*Now the Lord said to Samuel, "How long will you mourn for Saul, Seeing I have rejected him from reigning over Israel? Fill your horn with oil, and go; I am sending you to Jesse the Bethlehemite. **For I have provided Myself a king among his sons.**" And Samuel said, "How can I go? If Saul hears it, he will kill me." But the Lord said, "Take a heifer with you, and say, 'I have come to sacrifice to the Lord.' Then*

invite Jesse to the sacrifice, *and I will show you what you shall do;* **you shall anoint for Me the one I name to you.**" *So Samuel did what the Lord said, and went to Bethlehem. And the elders of the town trembled at his coming, and said, "Do you come peaceably?" And he said, "Peaceably; I have come to sacrifice to the Lord. Sanctify yourselves, and come with me to the sacrifice."* **Then he consecrated Jesse and his sons, and invited them to the sacrifice.** *So it was, when they came, that he looked at Eliab and said,* **"Surely the Lord's anointed is before Him!"** *But the Lord said to Samuel, "Do not look at his appearance or at his physical stature, because I have refused him. For the Lord does not see as man sees; for man looks at the outward appearance, but the Lord looks at the heart." So Jesse called Abinadab, and made him pass before Samuel. And he said, "Neither has the Lord chosen this one." Then Jesse made Shammah pass by. And he said, "Neither has the Lord chosen this one." Thus Jesse made seven of his sons pass before Samuel. And Samuel said to Jesse, "The Lord has not chosen these." And Samuel said to Jesse, "Are all the young men here?" Then he said, "There remains yet the youngest, and there he is, keeping the sheep." And Samuel said to Jesse, "Send and bring him.* **For we will not sit down till he comes here."** *So he sent and brought him in. Now he was ruddy, with bright*

*eyes, and good-looking. And the Lord said, **"Arise,*
anoint him; for this is the one!" Then Samuel took
the horn of oil and anointed him in the midst of his
***brothers;** and the Spirit of the Lord came upon David*
from that day forward. (1 Sam. 16:1–13, NKJV)

Imagine David watching over the sheep as a thirteen-year
old boy. Suddenly, he sees a servant running across the field
toward him. The young shepherd boy must have been puz-
zled or even fearful. The messenger wasn't carrying any food.
Was something wrong? We have no record of that conversation, but here is what we do know: the messenger would have
known that Samuel had invited the elders of Bethlehem to
attend a sacrifice to the Lord. This servant may have heard
Samuel say, "Are these all the sons that you have? Send for
him—we will not sit down until he arrives."

The entire family was waiting for David to arrive. Samuel
must have finished the sacrifice, as the elders were not present
when David showed up. David was probably anointed at
home, as the Lord determined to keep it a secret from Saul.
This was a once-in-a-lifetime opportunity for anyone. It was
an exclusive event, by invitation only. The impact on David's
spirit—seeing Samuel with his entire family waiting for him
to arrive—had to be both exciting and thought provoking.

Samuel refused to sit down until David came. As such,
David's value increased exponentially in the eyes of his
family. Samuel was very old at this point. We don't know the

details. Maybe the servant told David, "Run faster, Samuel will not sit until you come!" David may have been informed of these facts at the meal as the anointing oil was still dripping from his hair. Possibly Jesse told him after Samuel left. It isn't recorded, but David surely learned of it somehow. We can only imagine the impact on his life and the identity shift that resulted from that honor. Samuel celebrated David by his actions and words! David recognized that Father God had called him with such great honor from heaven. David responded with a life of worship.

It took more time to bring David than Samuel expected. Being quite old, he sat down to rest. When David—the forgotten shepherd boy shows up—the Lord tells Samuel to arise and anoint him. When David walked into the room, the man of greatest renown in the nation, accompanied by his entire family, stood to their feet. It released a celebration over David's life that molded his identity for God's purposes. We need to understand the value of celebrating people's lives with our actions. It releases honor that creates value. Honor unlocks the ability to dream with heaven. Conversely, dishonor is the enemy's attempt to stop or marginalize our value.

Samuel refused to eat the meal with Jesse and David's seven older brothers until David arrived. When a presidential meal is delayed until you arrive, it will shift you like it did David. I am sure that David wasn't seated in his normal place at the family table, but next to his father and Samuel. That is a "game changer" to anyone's identity! When we are seated in a new level of honor, we must receive it and live from it. The Father gave it to us for a purpose. God revealed David's destiny as the king of Israel with honor so that he could walk through the confusion and dishonor that he would encounter before his crown day. He gives us what we need to get through what we don't understand. With honor and celebration, Samuel released a dream into David's heart.

When I was twelve years old, I went forward in my church to give my life to Jesus. As I stood at the altar, the presence of God rained down on me in a way I had never experienced. I had a vision of myself, still twelve years old, speaking in front of a huge crowd of slightly younger Asians. Somehow, I knew they were Chinese. However, I simply thought this vision was my imagination. But after that I had an awesome encounter with the Lord in my second year of college, I shared that experience with some other students. One person said, "Dale that wasn't your imagination. God was showing you what you will be doing. Someday you will speak in China." Something in my spirit said "Amen." From that point on, I started carrying the dream for Asia in my heart.

Many years later I was invited to teach at Victory Bible Institute, a Chinese Bible school in Flushing, New York. I remember sharing my vision as I taught classes there for three years. There was a special anointing on the teachings as well as a wonderful presence of the Lord each time I heard the Chinese translator. I thought that I had fulfilled that vision.

Several years later another pastor heard my story and invited me to travel with his team to China. As the plane was landing in Beijing, I realized that through the classes I had taught, my voice had already been heard by college students in Beijing, as well as by many other Chinese-speaking people around the world. I shared my story with the Chinese believers that gathered for the meetings. "I saw you when I was twelve years old, but it took me forty years to get here—and now I am here living that vision." The same anointing that fell on me at twelve fell again on all of us in that room. When you live a dream, it sparks a dream in others.

Samuel was weeping when God told him to go anoint David. Samuel was grieving over the results of his ministry. Leaders and prophetic words only give opportunities—not guarantees. Guarantees are only obtained when those who are receiving promises connect to the Father who sent those words. Samuel wouldn't live to see his greatest prophecy fulfilled. Yet, the greatness of Samuel's life birthed the greatness in David's life. At significant times, God will send influential people into your life for impact and transition. God intentionally had Samuel anoint David as the future king in front of his father and brothers to shift his family's view of David, changing the atmosphere of his home.

All will never be happy, but most will be convinced. God will always allow an element of opposition to remain—it forces us to live in Him. Eliab was unhappy that David was chosen over him to be the next king of Israel. He despised and judged David at Goliath's challenge to Israel. Eliab said to David, "With whom have you left those few sheep in the wilderness?" (1 Sam. 17:28, NIV). Eliab was trying to devalue David in front of the other warriors, even in his capacity as a shepherd. The enemy will try to devalue our present activity as we are about to step into a new assignment. He questions our motivation and attacks our value in front of others. The enemy's greatest fear is that we will move into our position of greater purpose.

As David delivered food to his brothers, he found himself on Eliab's "turf." Eliab was trying to keep David out of the circle of influence he had created for himself among Israel's army. David may have been anointed king of Israel, but Eliab became territorial, and tried to block David's advancement. To be king during those times, you needed to be a fighting general who led the armies into battle. Saul rightfully questioned David's ability to fight Goliath. Goliath was infuriated that they would send a teenager to fight him. He felt dishonored. "Am I a dog that you come to me with sticks?" (17:43). Goliath didn't realize that he was facing the next anointed king of Israel.

The enemy was attacking David's identity before he even faced Goliath. The celebration that Samuel had released over David's life fortified David to navigate through these negative attitudes. David wasn't recognized as a warrior by others, but Samuel recognized more than a warrior in David. The identity shift that David experienced was more important than the victory over Goliath. Psalms is a book of praise, but

it is also a book of meditation. We must meditate on the celebrations that Father God has poured over our lives, as well as
taking our problems to Him. It keeps us living in the Father.
This was a major source of David's success.

Favor or Favoritism

God chose to write more about David's life than any other
person in the Bible. We can easily come to the conclusion that
David was God's favorite because of intangible qualities that
are out of our reach. We can disqualify ourselves from a life
of influence and greatness because we assume that we aren't
favored by God as David and other Bible greats were. Most
of them didn't see themselves as favored by God until He
spoke to them. Most struggled with who they were until God
changed their opinion and moved them into their new season.

Before studying David's life in depth, it would be easy to
conclude that God handed David such an incredible promise —
with guaranteed results — that he never struggled with his
identity. After all, David had faith and favor. He was a born
leader. Furthermore, he was handsome and athletic — humble
and patient. He was an anointed, gifted worshipper — a victorious, brave warrior. Reading the stories about David as
a young boy, it seemed to me that David started life with a
"silver sling and a golden harp" that caused him to be celebrated until he ascended Israel's throne. I assumed that David

had a major head start over the rest of us, but we have already addressed that misconception.

He was a man who had a heart after God—and that's God's opinion! *That had nothing to do with any of David's abilities, but rather his heart response to God.* That was the most important factor in David's life. Anyone can choose to pursue God with all their heart, soul, mind, and strength. If we choose that level of passion, it creates suffering. Often we conclude that a blessed life is an easy life. In fact, the opposite is true. Passion is a level of love that makes you willing to suffer to reach your goal. The root meaning of *passion* is "to suffer." The passion of an Olympic athlete results in purposeful and painful discipline to have the opportunity to win a gold medal. Jesus suffered to win. A blessed life exhibits faithfulness and fruitfulness in the midst of difficult situations.

We know the opposition David faced as Saul jealously hunted him down. We often focus on the amazing integrity and mercy in David's heart. Twice, he had the perfect opportunity to kill Saul—in self-defense no less! Yet, David refused to touch "the Lord's anointed," nor would he allow his men to do it for him.

Most people confuse favor with favoritism. We see favoritism throughout our lives, and call it favor. True favor is less seen and less understood, so it is easy to confuse with favoritism. Favor can also turn into favoritism over time— just as an intimate relationship with God can become distant.

Favor is based in God's love, and favoritism is based in our performance.

Favor is the tangible blessing of God's perfect love toward us that gives us opportunity to experience heaven's best. Favoritism, on the other hand, is an advantage gained by comparative performance. It allows you to receive the best things from other people—with the stipulation that you continue to perform as expected.

We are hurt by favoritism. We want it, yet we hate it. Favoritism is all too common in this broken world. Favoritism is ungodly, demonic, carnal, and a part of normal dysfunctional families. One finds it everywhere: in schools, in sports, in churches, and in politics. It is the golden ring people strain to grasp in this orphan world. Favoritism is so normal that even most Christians will think of it when favor is taught.

Those who enjoy favoritism must endure the ugly side of it as well: controlling demands, pressured performances, fear of rejection, and destructive pride. The loss of true love and a healthy identity is the price of favoritism. Man's love is easily corrupted by favoritism. It is possible that there is no love in pure favoritism. Favoritism is a form of acceptance apart from God's love. Favoritism is acquired by performance. It comes to those who are the most beautiful, the smartest, the strongest, the richest, the most talented, or the most powerful. There are very few of these "most" positions available in a crowded world. Favoritism creates a huge amount of rejection. Favor, however, is available for every person alive. Favor reveals the value that God has deposited in each life.

Favoritism demands that you continue to be the *most whatever* to enjoy your present status. Favoritism is a prison of fear built with marble and gold. Some call it a palace, but upon further inspection it is actually just a beautiful prison. Those who live in that palace/prison must make sure that no other orphans take their palace/prison from them. We must kill to remain in what is killing us.

Favoritism is created from need, but favor is created from a seed called love. Needs are intrinsically self-centered and selfish. We live from our need—or we live from a seed. If we don't live in God's love, our needs will become abusive to others. Favor transforms our lives into seeds from heaven to bless others. The key to obtaining favor in our life is birthed by our choice to give favor to others. God will bring special harvests of favor in strategic seasons in our life because of the seeds of favor we invested in those who could never help us in a previous season.

David sowed favor by the way he served his father who overlooked him. David didn't keep reminding his brothers of the great call on his life—he served them. We need to recall that he was bringing them food from home on the day he fought Goliath. Even though he was anointed to be the next king of Israel in front of all of his brothers, whom God didn't choose, he was still serving them. Unlike Joseph, David didn't antagonize his brothers by reminding them of his dreams. If you always speak of your dreams, it becomes very self-centered and toxic to friendships. Take interest in those God has placed in your life—ask questions and listen to their dreams.

Jacob put so much favor on Joseph, that Joseph's brothers couldn't remove it when they sold him into slavery. Potiphar couldn't remove it when he threw Joseph into prison after his wife lied about him. Our heavenly Father put so much favor on our life through Jesus Christ that no one or nothing can remove it if we receive that favor and keep willingly sowing it to others. Favor is more determined by how we treat others versus how people treat us.

In Acts 10:34–35 (NIV), Peter says, "I now realize how true it is that God does not show favoritism but accepts from every nation the one who fears him and does what is right." Peter is admitting he had a view of God that included favoritism based on the fact that he was Jewish. He didn't realize it was wrong until God confronted him in a vision. Then, God baptized the Gentile believers with the Holy Spirit to break the early church's attitude of favoritism towards Jewish believers that even existed among the first apostles. That attitude had been culturally entrenched in the apostles' lives as well as most of the Jewish people for ages.

What's my point? Favoritism was at the core of the early church, even as they were walking in miracles, signs and wonders. They weren't free from it, and neither are we. Peter's favoritism was based on hurts, persecutions, wars, personal experiences, and a limited understanding of God's actions. Favoritism is the number one enemy of favor! If the early church leaders hadn't shifted their thinking, the move of God would have been blocked by favoritism. Favoritism restricts God's people from freely receiving everything that He has for them. Favoritism ultimately tries to limit what heaven desires to accomplish on earth.

In contrast, consider the conversation Moses had with God in Exodus 33:12–13 (NIV). "Moses said to the Lord ..., 'You have said, "I know you by name and you have found favor with me." If you are pleased with me, *teach me your ways so I may know you and continue to find favor with you.* Remember that this nation is your people'" (emphasis added).

Favor is the gift of God's love from heaven. Moses knew the Lord was pleased with him, so he asked God to teach him His ways. God's ways reveal who He is. Moses wanted to know God so that he could keep His favor. Moses understood that favor was given freely, but that it was also extended and maintained through relationship. If we want to keep our spouse's favor, we must understand their ways. We will have to observe them and be taught by them—it doesn't come naturally. If we forget their ways, they will remind us. On a beautiful sunny day, my wife loves for us to go for a drive. Because of ministry trips, I can easily hit 30,000 miles a year. As such, going for a drive isn't my favorite way of relaxing after a long trip. However it still is one of the best ways I can bless her—which gains me favor. If shopping is included, it's double favor!

Similarly, if we desire favor with our boss—it's important to learn their ways. Then we won't lose the favor we have gained, but that favor will actually increase. It's important to do our job the boss's way instead of our way. The way something is done is very important when we are doing it for someone else. The manner in which something is done will not be overlooked by them—even in the midst of success. We honor that person when we do something their way. Permission should be sought if we think we have a better way of accomplishing the task. Favor from others hinges heavily on these truths.

We must understand God's ways so that we can please Him. He commands us to love our enemies, but He refuses to let us be people-pleasers. An overpowering desire to please others comes from a fear of rejection. In contrast, blessing others comes from knowing Him and His ways. Our eyes should be more on Him than on the person we are blessing. Our heart activity is more important to the Father than the actual results of an activity or interaction. Favor will never leave those who love like the Father. God extended His favor to us at the cross, but we must respond to Him to enjoy it.

David enjoyed a life of favor as he pursued God with all of his heart. David favored God, and God favored David. David would do whatever God asked of him. He honored God with his life. So God favored David and honored him beyond his expectations. David never expected that the coming Messiah would sit on his throne—the throne of David.

Chapter Three

HE RESTORES MY SOUL

The Lord is my shepherd; I shall not want. He makes me to lie down in green pastures; He leads me beside the still waters. He restores my soul; He leads me in the paths of righteousness for His name's sake. Yea, though I walk through the valley of the shadow of death, I will fear no evil; for You are with me; Your rod and Your staff, they comfort me. You prepare a table before me in the presence of my enemies; You anoint my head with oil; my cup runs over. Surely goodness and mercy shall follow me all the days of my life; and I will dwell in the house of the Lord forever. (Ps. 23, NKJV)

In David's most familiar Psalm, he reveals his intimate walk with God during the hard times. David understood "the valley of the shadow of death." Both Saul—his father-in-law, and Absalom—his very own son, hunted David down with their armies to kill him. When those closest to you are casting a shadow of death across you, it's difficult to overcome. You must live in the glory of your Father God to pass through those shadows of death. David said, "He restores my soul" (23:3). David escaped the shadow of death, but still his very soul needed ministry from God to recover fully.

Here, we clearly see that David is "saved" because the Lord is his shepherd. He even refers to the paths of righteousness, or personal holiness. God is showing David how to live. Yet David refers to the fact that God is restoring his soul. Our soul could be saved, but not restored from the trauma that we have endured. In the NIV translation it says "refreshed," and in the Living Bible, "strengthening."

Our soul contains our emotions. With one thought, the enemy can affect our emotions. The enemy strategically attacks our emotions through that one thought so he can gain greater access to our mind. Negative emotions and depression attack the truth to break the resolve of our decisions or our will. The enemy's goal is to limit us and our assignments. We can't let emotions rule our lives, but we don't ignore them either.

The joy of the Lord is our strength. His joy is the catalyst required to maximize the wisdom and power of His thoughts in your mind. It starts with the choice to give Him praise before the problem is eliminated. As we focus on Him with thanksgiving, we make God bigger and more important than our problem. As we worship, the Spirit of God will stir in us, releasing wisdom and authority to gain victory.

Man is spirit, soul, and body. Our spirit is more connected to our soul than to our physical body. When our spirit leaves our body, we are dead. Our soul departs with our spirit. Therefore, our soul is integrated within our spirit, and it has tremendous influence on our spirit. Our soul and spirit becomes the conduit through which the Holy Spirit moves. If our soul isn't restored, the Holy Spirit is restricted by the wounds in our soul that still remain.

Emotions have tremendous influence over the mind. Fear can cause a person to do something they have been trained not to do, or can hinder them from doing what they ought to do. In high-pressure or dangerous jobs, an employee must be trained and tested so that emotions don't affect their decisions. The employer understands that the natural response won't be the correct action required. God is strengthening our minds to prepare us for our future.

"The spirit of a man is the lamp of the Lord, searching all the inner depths of his heart" (Prov. 20:27, NKJV). Our spirit dwells in the Spirit of God and His Spirit also dwells in our spirit. It is a mystery that contains both elements. Christ lives in us, yet "in Him we live and move and have our being" (Acts 17:28).

The soul is our mind, will, and emotions. The restoring of our soul is a different and longer process than the saving of our soul. When Jesus saved our soul, we were qualified to enter heaven. As your soul is restored, it brings heaven to earth—the Father's love, wisdom and power. We must renew our mind for our emotions to be healed. We must break strongholds so that our mind can receive truth—then our spirit is freed. Ungodly beliefs can actually block us from living in the truth that we know.

When I was a young teenager, I was with my father as he was working underneath a truck from his business that had broken down. I had never helped him with mechanical repairs, and he was in a hurry to get the loaded truck back on the road. He asked me for a specific tool, but I was afraid to ask him to describe it as my eyes scanned through the toolbox. My father looked at me impatiently as he reached over and grabbed the tool from the toolbox to finish the task. I felt like he didn't have time for me and that I was in the way. My father probably never gave that event another thought, but it created a bitterroot expectation and an ungodly belief.

Years later when I became a pastor, I noticed that I always felt a bit uncomfortable and rushed in my sermon. It's not that I preached a shorter message, but that I felt an inner pressure that was always there. I felt that the congregation didn't have time for me and that I was in the way. I knew God had called me to preach and that the people had come to hear me, but my ungodly belief was hindering my call. After receiving counseling from Chester and Betsy Kylstra, I found it helpful to write the following three truths at the top of my sermon notes and repeat them quietly to myself before I preached:

1. The people want to hear what I have to say. I know what I am doing.
2. I am not in the way. I am right where I belong.

3. Father God is not rushing me to finish this service—
   enjoy Him. Talk slower.

It created a greater peace in me and in those listening. Not only did I enjoy preaching more, but it was also more effective—the peace allowed me to think more clearly as I preached. It's amazing how fear and rejection can steal or limit our gift. The Spirit of God leads us into all truth. The word of God is the path of truth that we walk by His Spirit.

The soul is a complex entity that is impossible to change without God's help and truth. The inner belief of the soul can actually be hidden from the mind. The soul can surprise a person when unexpected pressure releases emotions that give voice from the soul. As we listen to the emotional words that flood out from our soul, it can tell us things about ourselves that we may not know.

The best brain surgeons don't operate on themselves. It is important that we take time to receive ministry from others who are trained counselors. "Counselor" is one of God's names. It reveals an important attribute of Father God for our restoration. Similarly, even the best counselors understand themselves better with the help of another counselor. From time to time, set aside time to receive ministry from others. There would be fewer breakdowns if we would seek counsel to grow instead of just surviving the problem. God often uses problems to change us, but we normally just want Him to change what's around us—He accomplishes both.

Restoration adds value to everything it affects. It can make an $800 car worth $80,000! Restoration revitalizes identity and function. David experienced the restoration of his soul in his walk with God. It gave him the ability to respond to the leading of the Holy Spirit and to face the shadow of death without the fear of evil.

Processing Your Anger

"Be angry, and do not sin. Meditate within your heart on your bed, and be still" (Ps. 4:4, NKJV).

An unexpected flare up of anger can undo years of preparation or radically alter one's life course. We can't prepare for every situation, but as we invite the Lord to restore and strengthen our soul, we can move with the Spirit of God instead of responding from our wounds.

Anger is a helpful tool, much like pain. If we can't tell our doctor where it hurts and how it feels, it will be very difficult—if not impossible—for them to help us. When we are angry, scripture tells us to invite God's presence into that moment for understanding. He helps us to recognize the source of the hurt or fear that is producing that anger. We must dismantle fear and heal the hurt to keep anger from controlling our lives.

If we have no anger, then we are emotionally unhealthy. God *has* anger, but He *is* love. Anger is not a sin. Anger tells us something is wrong. A mother would use an "angry voice" to address her child who was about to run out in front of an oncoming truck. A voice of reason and love will not accomplish the necessary outcome in every situation. Anger has an element of warning that is contained in it. It lets us know that something in us or around us needs to stop now. Anger is like a fire alarm. It tells us something is burning and should be dealt with immediately before the fire rages out of control and destroys everything it touches.

> "*Be angry, and do not sin': do not let the sun go down on your wrath, nor give place to the devil*" (Eph. 4:26–27, NKJV).

It's surprising that we would be commanded to be angry, but cautioned not to sin. Then, God tells us that when anger arises it is time to be still. That is the last thing anger ever wants to do—*be still*. Ungodly anger demands its right to speak before thinking. Anger wants to be the god of your decisions. Through our stillness, we are choosing Him to be our God. As we meditate, God will reveal the source of our anger to us. This meditation could only take seconds, or could actually require weeks to process before speaking. Anger, when it is properly yielded to Him, will bring direction, revelation, and change. Process it and He will tell us what we are to do and say.

Jesus flipped the tables of the money changers—not the money changers. He drove them out with a whip, but he wasn't whipping them. There was anger in Jesus's zeal. This wasn't typical in His ministry, but it was a healthy "side street" He visited several times. We will only change what we desire or what disturbs us—normally they are intricately connected as one.

> *"Jesus put together a whip out of strips of leather and chased them out of the Temple, stampeding the sheep and cattle, upending the tables of the loan sharks, spilling coins left and right. He told the dove merchants, 'Get your things out of here! Stop turning my Father's house into a shopping mall!' That's when his disciples remembered the Scripture, 'Zeal for your house consumes me'" (John 2:15–17, MSG).*

In His zeal, there was a healthy anger that brought change to God's temple. This same zeal with healthy anger can bring change to our temple as well. It's time to meditate and process our anger so it doesn't turn into sin. If we don't process this anger before the Lord, Satan will take advantage of it and he will turn our anger into sin. If anger is suppressed, it will turn into depression and will explode at a time and in a way we do not desire.

When anger arises, please pray the following prayer first: "Holy Spirit, I invite you to reveal truth to me. In the name of Jesus, I bind the enemy from hiding truth or from blocking my journey to wholeness and healing. Lord Jesus Christ, I am asking You to restore my soul."

Meditations During Times of Anger

- Holy Spirit, what was done or said that triggered my anger in this current event?
- Holy Spirit, what is the core thought of my anger? It made me feel _____.
- Find the key phrases and write them down.
- What situation does this remind me of from my past?
- Holy Spirit, is this where it first started? Show me where.
- What did it make me feel like? (Identity issue)
- Holy Spirit, show me how these events are connected and similar.
- What ungodly belief has been created in my life? I believe that I will always _____.
- Renounce every spirit of fear, rejection, and abandonment.
- Ask the Holy Spirit to release His anointing into this particular area.
- What new godly belief based on scripture will I speak if I face the same situation?
- What actions do I see myself taking based on the new godly belief if there is a similar reoccurring event?
- What part of my identity was restored?

We have now created a new path for the Holy Spirit to lead us. As we are shifting in our mind, will, and emotions, our identity is also being restored. We can't simply remove an ungodly belief with an eraser. It takes a specific godly belief to displace a specific ungodly belief.

"So then, my beloved brethren, let every man be swift to hear, slow to speak, slow to wrath; for the wrath of man does not produce the righteousness of God" (James 1:19–20, NKJV).

The righteousness of God is graced with peace and love. Ungodly anger, which is fear based, is a major identity thief. If our soul is not restored, anger will erupt through those broken areas. Remember, anger tells us that something is wrong. Godly anger brings the needed change. We will remain angry or anger-prone if we will not deal with our issues.

Angry people use intimidation instead of authority to accomplish goals. Some people would not know how to approach life without anger. It's a tool they use to manipulate others. That spirit also manipulates those who use it. Ultimately, anger will destroy relationships as it distorts communication and removes the joy of life.

I pray that this would be the season where we gain authority over ungodly anger so that we can flourish in our God-given design. Give yourself the gift of forgiveness and then give it to others. This is a time to quiet our soul before our God and receive a fresh mantle. He has put greatness on the inside of us, but we must enter into that greatness by resting in Him. We can't take it; we must simply receive it. This is our time of transition from the wilderness of ungodly anger to our Promised Land that includes the zeal of God. There is a righteous anger that is essential to removing the giants from our Promised Land.

The Effects of Trauma

David enjoyed many extraordinary moments in his life that were absolutely breathtaking. But David also endured rejection and trauma that are almost inconceivable. This is very typical to all mankind. Jesus said, "Let the little children come to Me" (Matt. 19:14). While we were children, Jesus released the Father's love into our lives to position us to trust Him for greater things He has planned for us. Conversely while we are children, the enemy sets fear and rejection against us to limit our ability to trust God as we grow closer to our destiny.

"This will be worse for you than all the calamities that have come on you from your youth till now" (2 Samuel 19:7, NIV).

In the above verse, Joab is talking with David after Absalom was killed and his rebellion quelled. Joab, David's nephew, knew of the calamities that had befallen David from his youth. David was called to be a public leader, and most of his tests were in the eye of the public. You are tested in the sphere of your authority and purpose.

Let's look at the traumas that David faced on his journey to becoming king. He was overlooked by his Father and was despised by his oldest brother. King Saul loved David greatly (1 Samuel 16:21 NKJV). If we overlook this fact, we will not grasp the weight of the trauma that David had to overcome as Saul tried to destroy him. While David was playing his harp for the king of Israel—who was his father-in-law—Saul tried to pin David to the wall with his spear.

When David killed Goliath, we have no record of him receiving the promised financial reward or the removal of land taxes for his family. When Saul offered David his second daughter in marriage, David referred to himself as a "poor man" (1 Sam. 18:23, NIV). David's promised wife and his actual wife, the two daughters of the king, were both taken from him and given to other men. Abigail became David's wife as he was fleeing from Saul. Michal was only returned to David shortly before he was made king over Israel.

David led the armies of Israel into battle, and then was pursued by those same armies. David defeated the Philistines, but then he was forced to hide among them to escape Saul's sword. These factors had all the ingredients to sink David into a deep depression. David didn't cave into depression, but it produced a sense of instability. The scripture tells us that David perceived that God had *established* him as king. There comes a point in time that we must comprehend that God has established us. Stability is a very important component of destiny.

David mentored the mighty men that came to him at the cave of Adullam. When they returned to Ziklag tired from the long journey, they found the town burned to the ground—their wives, children and possessions were gone! The men were so discouraged that they talked among themselves about killing David. God brought David to a place where no one believed in him, and where he was personally discouraged as well. God will bring us into a place where we can only lean on Him. It sets us apart as leaders to work with others on a higher level of authority and honor. It is a prerequisite for all of those whom God will entrust with thrones of authority to shift the earth. David did not just survive Ziklag. He led those that were talking of killing him into a major miraculous victory!

When David was anointed as king in Judah, it started a civil war in the nation. How could David deal with the fact that his destiny to lead his nation was ripping it apart through civil war? While he was the king of Judah, David had to live with the burden of Israel's rejection over the following seven-and-a-half years—that's a long time with no change. Partial success can forge frustration, causing many to walk away during the last phase that precedes fulfillment.

All the trauma and drama that came against David required great tenacity and passion for him to possess what God had promised. Traumas and drama are the number-one destroyers of identity if we let them dominate us. We must focus on the dream and let it carry us past the trauma of a jealous brother and a leader who desires our ruin. David's choices elevated him and developed the strength in his life required for those who are called to be kings. Our godly response to ungodly trauma is our access to our next level of authority. The cross was the trauma Jesus chose to endure to free us from it, and then He ascended to His throne!

We tend to overlook the myriad of traumatic events that David endured, as well as the toll they took on his soul. David endured more trauma than most people in the Bible. I believe that David suffered in more ways than Joseph, and was closer to Job than we may realize. Job's test only lasted a short time, but it was severe. There is no way to determine who suffered the most. Pity will never carry healing—it only brings attention. Love, however, carries healing.

Trauma becomes a gateway to unreasonable fears that limit us and drastically affect our decisions. Traumas produce and reinforce negative views of our identity and destiny. These negative thoughts create strongholds to bind us from natural spiritual growth. This restricts our authority, purpose, and fruitfulness. These negative thoughts paint a picture of our life that is filled with defeat and rejection. Trauma is sent from the enemy to create a negative identity—*to steal our destiny*. It normally starts with one thought that becomes the root issue. Out of this one thought, negative attitudes are birthed toward God, others, and ourselves. Reoccurring events that are connected to the same issue reveal the need for healing and deliverance from that bitter-root expectation.

Most traumatic events contain an element of insanity, because it is illogical and unexpected to the victim. People will even say, "That's insane!" The mind can break or become weakened when it struggles to process illogical events. Those thoughts can take on a life of their own that is difficult to control or stop. It can steal the inner rest a person needs, and can even block the ability to sleep. The enemy attempts to steal from us any joy that could be left in life. He is very oppressive.

When something is illogical, there is often a demonic force behind it. The depression and fear that affects a person's mind and spirit becomes a major battleground. God wants to detach our heart from those traumatic events so they don't control or influence us. Look at the trauma Jesus endured on the cross to bring healing to our heart. Like David, allow the Good Shepherd to choose the times that He makes us lie down in the green grass by the river of life to restore our soul.

Someone once asked me, "Why dig up dead horses?" First of all, they aren't dead—they are simply in your past. They are still hitched to your life, and they are dragging you away from your destiny. Not thinking about them won't make them go away. I want you to disconnect from those "horses," and put them to rest so you can live unhindered by them.

In the Bible, "heart" is sometimes used interchangeably with "mind." "Heart" also speaks of emotions and will. It's easy to see that the heart carries the components of your soul.

We often speak of Jesus living in our heart. The heart is also the place Jesus desires to heal and restore. The deeper the healing of your heart, the more God can flow through your heart and life. I call it "power living from the heart."

"Keep your heart with all diligence, for out of it spring the issues of life" (Prov. 4:23, NKJV).

Solomon exhorts us to keep watch over our heart. When the Lord reveals a heart issue, He does so in His timing to see it healed so we can continue our journey into our destiny. We are not responsible until He brings it up. If we can't trust our heart, we must control our broken heart with our carnal mind. That produces a tense, tired life. A renewed mind would be equal to a restored heart. What we are speaking of here is a legalistic mind trying to control a carnal heart so that it won't do the wrong thing. This is life in its worst form. We would be reduced to a carnal, mind-controlled life rather than a Spirit-led life. Joy, wisdom, and power will flow as we live from the heart of God with a renewed mind.

"A good man out of the good treasure of his heart brings forth good; and an evil man out of the evil treasure of his heart brings forth evil. For out of the abundance of the heart his mouth speaks" (Luke 6:45, NKJV).

When the treasure of our heart reaches the point of abundance, we will bring forth good or evil with the words we speak. Without abundance, there will be no speaking or decreeing. When we speak, we release the abundance of the treasure that is in us to others. I find it interesting that both evil and good live out of the treasure of one's heart. The treasures of heaven will overflow from our heart when it reaches the point of abundance. That kind of life has the power to shift earth!

> *"And when He had removed him, He raised up for them David as king, to whom also He gave testimony and said, 'I have found David the son of Jesse, a man after My own heart, who will do all My will'" (Acts 13:22, NKJV).*

David pursued the heart of God until God's heart was in David's heart. Out of David's life, the heart of God was revealed in many aspects. God described David as someone who would do everything I asked of him. David was responsive to God's requests. David's worship was not only in his songs, it was also expressed in his life. Our desire and obedience to do our Father's will is our worship. David was a man after Father God's heart by what he did for Father God. The heart of God is a way of thinking and living.

I was waiting in an airport for my flight to depart, and the Lord directed me to encourage a woman nearby. It interrupted my negative attitude, so I repented quietly as I stepped over to speak to her. She wept as I gave her the words of life, and then she thanked me. As I walked away, I asked the Lord why He chose me for that assignment. "Didn't you see what was in my heart?" He said words I will never forget: "I knew you would do it for Me." Those words brought such a joy to my heart. Then He continued speaking: "You were the best thing I had available within fifty feet." My joy turned to laughter.

How did David come into such a deep pursuit of God's heart? After David was anointed by Samuel, he continued watching the sheep, playing his harp, and developing a deep worship life. The anointing of Samuel's life as a young boy in the presence of the Lord in the temple was now on David in the fields. David stirred the anointing and intimacy with the Father until it was birthed in him. David's worship flowed into the book of Psalms.

David loved the Lord with all his heart, soul, mind, and strength—he connected to the Father as he worshiped and meditated. There are certain things no natural father can transfer to his son. Those things can only be received directly from the heavenly Father. Jesus told His disciples to call no man "father" (Matt. 23:9), even though He also said previously that we are to honor our father and mother (Matt. 15:4). He was revealing the true relationship that we have with God.

"Then the word of the Lord came to me, saying: 'Before I formed you in the womb I knew you; Before you were

*born I sanctified you; I ordained you a prophet to the
nations.'" (Jeremiah 1:4–5 (NKJV).*

We came from God, our Father, through our parents. Our
parents were the natural doors that God chose to bring us to
earth. God knew us before we were in our mother's womb.
Our parents didn't know us then. Father God created us;
our parents birthed us. If we truly see God as our Father, it
will help us to receive from Him as a son. Our identity is
unleashed when we truly see God as our Father and ourselves as His sons. Many simply look at their natural parents,
trying to determine their value and future. Honor them, but
look beyond them to "our Father" and gain a new perspective. It shifts the way we approach God when we see him as
our Father. All of our needs take on a different expectation
because of that relationship. The nature and words of our
prayers will change as that relationship grows closer.

Insecurity — The Enemy of Destiny

Insecurity resists the new, even though it may dream of it.
Insecurity demands that we cling to what we have because of
fear of loss. It may even tempt a person to take what someone
else has already obtained, because it doesn't have the confidence and vision to create destiny. Insecurity is a thief,
a deceiver, and an accuser. Insecurity is a spirit, a way of
thinking, and a view of life that everyone must overcome.

Lucifer couldn't overcome it. Love casts out fear (1 John 4:18). Fear, the lack of love, is the root of insecurity. Father God's love eliminates insecurity and brings amazing confidence to His sons. Security that rests on accomplishments alone can be stolen in a moment. Security must be deeply rooted in our relationship with God as our Father. His security with past victories gives us the platform to risk greater vision.

Fear of loss is a mean boss. It actually infringes on healthy growth and fulfillment of goals. Vision decrees that we are moving into our destiny, stewarding what we had in the last season in a new way. Ditching our responsibilities of the past season reveals irresponsibility and a lack of wisdom that will follow us into our next season. The old season isn't the problem any more than the new season is the answer. We must live in His presence—don't try to escape into the future or hide in the past. Walking with God is more important that rushing to our destination. Enjoy the journey! When we have reached our throne destination, new assignments will be given. David never envisioned building the temple after defeating Goliath. That desire was birthed after becoming king. David raised the money, drew up the designs, and chose the craftsmen for the temple that God would not let him build. Solomon actually built David's temple.

New is unfamiliar and unknown. It is a source of discomfort and risk. *New* is disorganized, uncharted, unfinished, and more challenging than the old. It requires new growth and a more determined resolve to deal with the greater problems that accompany greater goals. It often requires more money than we presently have. New is not for the lazy or uncommitted. New requires more work to initiate. It will be accompanied by new favor from new people in new circles. God is about to do more *new* in us so He can do more *new* through us.

Godly confidence and vision keep us moving from one phase of our lives into the next one. Most phases must be completed before we move forward into the next phase. Completing a season should not be judged by perfectionism or idealism. An accomplished goal is completed with faith and excellence. Satisfaction is gained in thankfulness and realistic assessment of life goals. Father God said, "For I am the Lord, I do not change" (Mal. 3:6). Nonetheless, the God who doesn't change brings changes to us and to everything around us.

Destiny and insecurity are incompatible. We must deal with the fear of the unknown. In order to stop us, the enemy designs circumstances and manipulates attitudes in others to create fear in us. In the midst of the enemy's plans, God designs His tests and purposes to invite us to move into a higher level in Him and our destiny. Then like Joseph we can declare that what the enemy intended for evil, God used for good (Gen. 50:20). If Joseph had become bitter and insecure, nothing good would have come out of the evil his brothers did to him. Had he killed his brothers, enslaved them, or ignored them—Israel wouldn't exist today.

Insecure areas in our lives are like magnets that continue to attract challenges until we mature emotionally. This allows us to reflect Christ in a greater glory and more accurately. If we fear those in authority, we present ourselves in such a way that they will fulfill our expectations. Just as an angry person yelling stirs up fear and anger in those around them, a person with deep rejection will also stir up rejection. Life events and relationships provide us the opportunities we need to mature, overcome fears, and gain new faith and godly expectations.

Did the enemy design the tests for Joseph, or was God a major player in designing those tests to help Joseph qualify for his palace dream? The Bible clearly states that God will not allow the enemy to tempt us beyond that which we can endure (1 Cor. 10:13). The scriptures also mention that God didn't drive out all of Israel's enemies so that He could test them—so they could know what was in their heart (Judg. 3:1–4). Father God already knew, but they did not. When Father God reveals something that is hidden in your heart, it is His timing and design to propel you forward.

Chapter Four

TRAINED AND MENTORED

If we needed a complicated surgery, would we choose an atheist who was the foremost specialist in their field, or a Christian general practitioner who had been our best friend for years? Would we desire trained expertise or the faith of a friend? Personally, I would have my Christian doctor friend praying for me while the atheist expert operated. As a patient, we want a miracle from the operation, not a miracle that the doctor could finish the operation. Some people expect that God will bless them where they haven't been trained and haven't had prior success simply because they are Christians.

Success does not come without the help or instruction from someone who has succeeded. Normally, God doesn't call people without experience to accomplish a specific task. There are exceptions when it is a unique situation, but it isn't the standard of God's kingdom. Noah was not chosen because of prior boat building experience. When God calls us, He qualifies us for that call. Moses was saved for a special day and trained as well. He was raised to lead in the palace of Egypt, so leading Israel was within his training. The greater the call, the greater the training and tests will be. Previous success precedes a greater call. We can't quit in the middle of that hard test, it is qualifying us for greatness.

Would we want to be the first passenger to ride on an untested airplane design, flown by a young trainee pilot and a retired lawyer co-pilot that had dreamed of flying his entire life? Father God's wisdom exceeds that of the airplane industry. God's kingdom will be accelerated by trained visionary sons who will build the designs of heaven for their Father God on earth. Moses not only received the Ten Commandments, he received the design of heaven to build a place on earth where men could meet and worship Father God. He had to remember numerous specific details and measurements. Moses was raised and schooled in the courts of Pharaoh that built the astounding pyramids with mathematical expertise that still puzzles our present day intelligence. His education in Egypt was not wasted when he was chosen by God to build the Tabernacle.

It is crucial to train with experienced leaders to gain spiritual knowledge and practical life wisdom. Each of us needs hands-on training and shared experiences with mentors. David learned to be a warrior and a king as he observed Saul. David received a worship mantle when Samuel anointed young David to be king. David received from great men, to become great.

Before David became king, he raised up the discouraged and the discontent that were willing to join David while he was on the run from King Saul to save his life. These men were also visionaries. This is often overlooked. They knew David and believed that God had chosen him to be king. They joined him when there was nothing to gain and everything to lose.

These men became the greatest warriors in all the history of Israel. They killed giants and were victorious in the face of insurmountable situations. Why? They were trained by a giant killer. David taught them valor by the way he honored King Saul when he was hunted by him. It is interesting to me that none of these great warriors ever turned on David personally, because they followed David's example. Father God always calls us individually, but he trains us with others.

David also had some wicked and worthless men fighting alongside the great men. These wicked and worthless men—that fought the battle after the raid upon Ziklag—did not want to share the spoils with the two hundred that were too tired to pursue the enemy. (1Sam. 30:22) David would not allow their attitudes to divide his limited troops and reminded them that it was God who gave them the victory. Your troop will never be purer than David's—people will still want to take the credit and determine the rewards for others. Step up David and keep the unity in the midst of victory. Some who were out of it yesterday—are needed tomorrow. God also used those wicked and worthless men to help David win, but David could not allow them to determine the policy.

Hurts and offenses occur in the mentoring process because the enemy is trying to separate fathers from sons. His goal is to stop the process that empowers the next generation. There is no place on earth to be trained where hurts and disappointments will not occur at some level. Hurts and disappointments are the core elements of abuse. They will be the result of inattentiveness and imperfections that we each have. Rules and guidelines that were intended to help us—also have the ability to hurt us. Until someone is disappointed with a leader or their decision, their commitment to that leader is untested. When you disagree and remain faithful in your service while honoring your leaders, you have achieved a "Davidic" victory that will open many doors for you and your destiny. Imperfections will also help the sons not to "worship" their fathers, but rather to truly honor them.

The enemy will try to discourage fathers from the process so the next generation does not carry the anointing to finish what God has started through them. Father God has nothing to do with hurt, but He promised the comfort of the Holy Spirit for the hurts that are very uncomfortable. As you look to Him and His love, He builds something special in your life because you trusted Him *beyond* the hurt. Abuse touches each life and through each life in some fashion. The devil is evil, and the enemy works through people. More often than you might believe—their part is hidden from their eyes. The angriest child makes the worst Father. Guard your heart—insure your future—fathers are needed ahead.

People who are hurt and angry rarely remember what they said. On several occasions I had members and even leaders in my church who were angry send me emails or letters. After most of the emotions had settled, I referred back to statements that they wrote to me as I was restoring the person and the relationship. Several denied making those statements and I felt they were being truthful. They did not believe me until they read their letters that I had saved. The enemy was speaking through their hurts and fears, but those thoughts — most often — were not in their heart. Don't take it personally as a leader. The enemy was moving thorough their broken emotions and unresolved issues of their past to connect to one of yours.

When I meet people and hear their stories from their childhood — especially stories that pertain to their parents — I know it will affect our relationship down the road if we remain close. The specific unresolved issues they had with their father I will face with them in the future — because I am a father. The details and circumstances recreate the setting where the problem started. One close leader in my church had struggled often with me as he did with his father. However, he never had any issues with my wife. As he was getting ready to work with her, I commented jokingly to him that now he was about to face his unresolved issues with his mother. He did not believe me until after six months of working with my wife on a project. The issues we did not resolve in our childhood, we will have a chance to complete with our spouse, close friends or other authority figures in our life.

When we are hurt by close friends, we doubt God's ways and inwardly vow to never trust people again. That is the enemy's goal. He knows that you cannot fulfill your destiny without trusting God and people. Jesus poured His life into twelve men, knowing the very one who would betray Him, and then left earth trusting them to build His church. You must pour out your best even when betrayal is present or possible.

Only Jesus was perfect, so we must all recognize that each of us has hurt others in some fashion. As we forgive others and repent, we stay aligned with God's heart and our destiny journey. Repentance is where our walk started with God, and it is what keeps our walk with Him strong.

Each stage in our life's journey is designed by God to increase our wisdom and our gifts, as well as to refine our character. There are "vision updates" and "heart tests" at each stage. God will also refine small insecurities and negative identity issues to the deepest level by allowing increasingly challenging tests at every stage of our journey. If we are seated in heavenly places the unexpected turbulence will not overwhelm us!

Many people are disheartened when they face the same issue they thought they'd conquered in the last season. However, they're not just circling the mountain, they are climbing the mountain. They are now able to receive a deeper healing for that same issue. The past victory stands, but now they are facing another challenge at higher place on their mountain. In His love, God didn't allow a dozen major issues to invade our life. Most people usually have to confront one issue that has two major supporting issues that produce many branches. This is an oversimplification of a complicated subject.

David's ability to shift seasons during his journey was one of the major factors that gave him the testimony that he served God's purpose in his own generation (Acts 13:36). Wounds and offense are the main reasons why we are stuck in the last season.

We often reminisce about our experiences. These events include both the wonderful and the terrible, as they are the most memorable. We should be able to discern if we are emotionally stuck in the past by the way we tell those stories. Did our body tense up as we talked? Did our heartbeat increase? Did we speak louder or faster? Did it stir up painful thoughts and emotions? We should not be hard on ourselves. All wounds take time to heal. Is the pain less now since the last time we told that story? Good. God is restoring our soul. We are maturing and healing. I was telling someone a very painful event in my life and it seemed as if I was almost talking about another person's life. All the emotions that I normally experienced over the years, that were continually diminishing each time as I told that story, were gone. It surprised me and I was so thankful to the Lord.

David handled most hurts in his life with truth and healthy emotions. Yet one event David never negatively responded to when it occurred, ended up being a major stronghold over his life. He was emotionally stuck on one traumatic event from his past; Saul gave his daughter Merab—who was promised to David—to another man on David's wedding day. We see the hurt from the trauma manifest in his angry, judgmental response to Nathan's parable. (2 Samuel 12) Nathan responds by saying, "You are the man!" David had done what he bitterly judged and refused to forgive. What King Saul did to David when he was a king, David did to Uriah when he was king. The consequences of his affair with Bathsheba—which cost him dearly—were more about unforgiveness and judgment toward Saul than the lust that was present. God is committed to dealing with any self-righteous spirit in His favored sons and daughters. He wants nothing blocking our hearts from His. It is easier for our Father God to handle our failures than our self-righteousness or pride—one is an event, the other is the tone of our relationship with Him.

Lackadaisical or overly driven lives are indicators of being stuck in the past. One is immobilized by the past—the other is driven to remove the pain of the past with present victories. Vision is designed for Father God's glory, not personal pain reduction. Victories will lessen the pain of the past, but that is not its purpose in God's Kingdom. Destiny lives in the present, pressing toward tomorrow. Faith is now—pain is the past. Pain produces fear of the future. Destiny has an underlying sense of joy and expectation. Healing is coming to us as we pursue the Lord and embrace the dream. Carry the dream until the dream carries you.

Shifts

David experienced major shifts in his life to reach his destiny. Let's review his life briefly. David started as a shepherd. His lot in life seemed ordinary, and his future easily predictable. He probably dreamed of being a shepherd, as any son of a shepherd would have, until Samuel released God's dream into his heart. It's amazing how many extraordinary lives starts off in a very ordinary mundane fashion. God is a dream changer, game changer.

At the age of thirteen, David was anointed by Samuel to be the next king of Israel. Saul had been king for twenty-three years. Can you imagine some of the conflicting thoughts that entered David's mind from this unexpected shift to his future? David's vision transferred from the sheep of his father, to the sheep of Israel. Since Samuel came to him in secret, David could not share that dream with others. Another seventeen years would pass before David would be crowned king of Judah. God intended that David continue working as a shepherd with a "king" dream. David received revelation that the Lord was his shepherd—as he watched over the flock.

Everyone has the ability to rise to greatness because they were made in the image of God and have a creative imagination. No one in the Bible accomplished great things without God speaking to them—*and about them*. "Dream seeds" are sown into our hearts by people we meet or needs we see. They can rise in us as we read about a person in scriptures or in other books. The seeds of destiny start to take root as we desire to please God with our life. To enter into our destiny, it is critical that we passionately pursue and embrace the things God has placed inside of us. Every vision requires unending patience and relentless pursuit.

After David embraced the word of the Lord, he had to go back to shepherding the sheep. David had to continue with the ordinary while entertaining the extraordinary. This dynamic tension must be endured for us to enter into the greatness of our call. We must keep the vision alive through parallel realities. Our present activity is developing a skill set and a maturity that is required for our future. There comes a time in our life when all of our seasons and acquired wisdom come into a dynamic convergence.

The Holy Spirit rested upon David when he was anointed by Samuel. That anointing empowered David to kill a lion and a bear. This is a daring accomplishment for a man—inconceivable for a youth! This was not a result of David's ability, but rather God's empowering anointing that rested on his life. The anointing to be king was transforming the shepherd boy. This is an important key to attaining destiny. God is watching to see if you do the ordinary in an extraordinary way while your destiny and identity is still hidden.

Everyone receives "prophetic" words from others that contain unique parts of their destiny. It may be practical advice or amazingly anointed words. These words create key pieces of your destiny that come together like a puzzle. To reach your destiny, you must gain insight from each piece from numerous seasons.

One of Saul's servants had this to say about him: "Behold, I have seen a son of Jesse the Bethlehemite who is a skillful musician, a mighty man of valor, a warrior, one prudent in speech, and a handsome man; and the LORD is with him." (1 Sam. 16:18, NIV).

This is a very interesting list. David was not just a musician, he was a skillful musician. He practiced to be skillful. As David was being recommended for a minstrel position, his skill level was mentioned first—not the presence of the Lord in his life. The presence of the Lord was more important, but it will not qualify David for this opportunity. Because he played skillfully unto the Lord in the fields, it landed him a job playing for the king in the palace. In Colossians 3:23, Paul challenges us to "work heartily, as to the Lord." If we do so, it births a spirit of excellence that cooperates with God's chosen promotions for our lives. Add skill to the anointed gifts in your life—it will take you places.

He was a man of valor. Valor is an old-fashioned word that means "strength of mind or spirit that enables a person to encounter danger with firmness; personal bravery." David demonstrated a commitment level in his life responsibilities that was extraordinary. He gave diligence to that which seemed unimportant. How we do anything determines how we do everything.

David was a warrior. He knew how to fight the good fight of faith. *He was not afraid of the risk of battle*. There are many battles on the road to destiny that the faint-hearted will not face or overcome. There are decision battles and the rejection wars that we must all face to enter and maintain our destiny. Since there is no record of any battles David had fought at this point in time, the young servant must have known about the lion and the bear and recognized the warrior ability in David. These remarks were made by someone who knew David well.

David was prudent in speech. He showed good, careful judgment. David was a wise communicator who knew when and how to speak. He also knew when to remain silent. Being prudent in speech, will open doors of destiny. Foolish speech or overstated opinions will slam the doors shut. The *need to be right* is the death of greater influence as it is based in insecurity and false identity. How we handle truth determines if others will listen. If we need to say everything we know at anytime, we will not be given entrance to a palace.

David was also good looking. This comment goes beyond his good looks and speaks of his personal cleanliness in a job that made it difficult. David carried himself well before others. David was a good fit and a great addition in the king's palace. We must learn to live above our circumstances and plausible excuses.

Most importantly, the Lord was with David. The mastery of the harp and the anointing that rested on David's life caused the evil spirits to depart from Saul. This would not have been possible without both of these elements linked together. David's lifestyle of worship in the fields opened up the doors to the palace.

David became one of Saul's armor-bearers (1 Sam. 16:21). David was advancing into the words that Samuel had spoken over him. David could have easily settled for just being an anointed worship leaders, but he wouldn't have fulfilled his calling. David was now being groomed as a warrior. David never lost the worship anointing that God instilled in him as a young shepherd boy. David's heart of worship defined his life and his reign.

David had a coveted position in Jerusalem serving the king, but he still served his aging father by looking after the sheep. David lived a balanced life in the midst of great promotion and extraordinary opportunities. David exemplified a faithful life in his patience journey toward his destiny — yet he possessed the zeal needed to reach it. David knew how to seize the day. David wasn't bashful or backwards! His life was not imprisoned with false humility or unworthiness. David lived as a son linked into his Father God's greatness. David expected great things in his life. Do we?

Jesse sent David to his brothers to see how they were faring and to get a report how the battle was going. David was also delivering bread to his brothers and cheese to the commanders on the front lines. David's brothers were war-riors in the army of Israel—yet David was closer to the king than they were. Even though he was anointed above his brothers, he served them at his father's request. David deliv-ered the bread and cheese to the keeper of the supplies before he entered the battlefield with Goliath. David never tried to "jump-start" his calling—nor did he run from it. He didn't lord it over his brothers, who knew he had been anointed as king of Israel—instead David served them. How we serve will determine how we will lead—and who will follow us. Many people plan to do more and be more, when they reach their destiny. Remember, what we do when we are "not there" determines if we get there.

Some people don't serve well at a lower level because they are so focused on their high calling that they become self-centered—forgetting to serve others. David knew how to live each day unto the Lord while pursuing his calling. Don't be overly critical of those who have entered into a high level of success. Success is more difficult to manage than most think. It's easier to get back up when we fall, than to remain low when the Lord lifts us up. Great success presents greater challenges that require constant growth for longevity.

Upon killing Goliath, David instantly became a national hero and launched his career as a military leader. From that day forward Saul kept David with him and did not let him return to his father's house. There are pivotal victories that change our life forever. We cannot go back to what we did and where we lived, because we have been repositioned by someone in greater authority. What raised us up could become counterproductive to our journey into destiny if we refused to shift in our day of promotion. This was at King Saul's request, not David's. An environmental shift was needed at this time in David's life to intensify his training for the call. God moved David from the fields of Jesse to the palace of the king.

David experienced numerous shifts at personal and professional levels during this season of his life. He was enlisted in the king's service. Then he married the king's daughter. He was now active in the palace with the "First Family"—living very close to the king. He shifted from eating with his father to eating at the king's table. He was no longer watching the sheep, but leading the armies. Even so, David was not prideful, nor apologetic. He fully and quickly embraced these shifts. This is not as easy as it seems.

A healthy identity is required to make these shifts. Integrity determines if we will maintain the purpose of the promotion. We are elevated to help others—not ourselves. Our journey should create a path for others to follow. David was God's answer to help Israel come back to Him in true worship.

The Expectation of Reward

Then David spoke to the men who were standing by him, saying, "What will be done for the man who kills this Philistine and takes away the reproach from Israel? For who is this uncircumcised Philistine, that he should taunt the armies of the living God?" The people answered him in accord with this word, saying, "Thus it will be done for the man who kills him." Then he turned away from him to another and said the same thing; and the people answered the same thing as before. When the words which David spoke were heard, they told them to Saul, and he sent for him. (1 Sam. 17:26, 27–30, 31)

David had a godly expectation of a reward for his victory. Twice, he asked about the reward for the man who would win the battle. David had a winner's mentality before he entered the battle. He saw himself victorious before he ran toward Goliath. I never understood David's motivation for asking about the reward twice. I was raised in a church that taught God was a rewarder of those who were faithful and obedient. This reward would be received in heaven, not here on earth.

Yet from Genesis onward, we see God blessing people as they lived their life on earth. Possessions and wealth in many churches were associated with those who didn't love

God or simply carnal Christians. If a believer had a very nice car, they were thought to be backslidden and prideful. You could buy a Chevrolet or possibly a Buick, but a Cadillac definitely wasn't on the list. Was God tempting Abraham to backslide by making him rich and powerful? No. Abraham had a very unique goal with his expectation of prosperity. After a battle, Abraham wouldn't take one sandal from the king of Sodom so that no one could say, "I have made Abram rich." (Gen. 14:23) Abraham expected to be rich, and his testimony was going to be that God alone had orchestrated it. We need more good old-fashioned believers like Abraham to rise up! Abraham was also willing to leave it all and go to a land that the Lord had not yet showed him. Abraham was willing to give up everything to follow the Lord and yet believe for great wealth.

Look at the great riches David had amassed at the end of his life. In 1 Chronicles 28–29, we see he very generously gave resources needed to build the temple of God. He was the largest giver. God restored to David—above and beyond—for what Saul didn't give him for defeating Goliath. A godly rich person is not known by the wealth they have obtained, but by the faith through which that wealth was attained—as well as by their generosity. By these principles, there are people earning minimum wage who are "wealthier" than some millionaires. Those who hoard and never give to help others have been overtaken by a spirit of poverty and greed. Greed is not limited to the wealthy. It can enslave the poorest person.

God rewards His servants to reveal God's heart and character. His rewards are more about who He is and how He operates rather than those receiving them. Would we work for a company that refused to pay us? I don't think so. It would speak poorly of that company. Don't we think God operates at a higher standard than a fortune 500 corporation? If God doesn't reward us here on earth, how could we believe that He will reward us when we get to heaven? God's nature is consistent in time and in eternity—He changes not.

A pastor in Taiwan asked me if I believed in sacrificing it all for the Lord or believing for prosperity. The scriptures teach each of these aspects, so I believe every believer should experience both of them. They can also be two different seasons in your life as Paul referred to in scripture. In the book of Acts it is recorded that they gave houses and land to the apostles, yet they met house to house. People did not become homeless because of their giving. They gave out of their prosperity with a willing heart.

When we see another brother in abundance, rejoice with him in his blessing as if it were yours! It breaks through fear of lack or jealousy and releases greater faith to usher in our blessings. We are not blessed until we have enough to help someone else. This is a heart issue and it is not connected to our bank balance. When you feel like you have nothing, it is a good time to help someone else.

Some think that abundance for one person is based on someone else's lack. So if we do not pursue abundance, it will help someone else have more. We act as if Father God only has ten biscuits and twelve sons. That means that two sons will not have anything to eat at each meal, unless someone eats less and shares. If we are to succeed with this mentality, we must secure the first biscuit to survive. Yet we really need an extra biscuit or two if we are to get ahead in life—and if we share we will never succeed.

Jesus fed a multitude from one boy's lunch. Abundance occurred when that boy brought what little he had to Jesus. Sharing should start when we have little. It crushes the spirit of greed. Remember they gathered twelve baskets after everyone had eaten their fill. That's our Father's economy!

> *"And without faith it is impossible to please Him, for he who comes to God must believe that He is and that He is a rewarder of those who seek Him" (Heb. 11:6, NASB).*

It is interesting to note the scripture says that without faith it is impossible to please God. This faith includes believing that God is and that He is a rewarder. Jesus even said, "Because you have seen Me, you have believed. Blessed are those who have not seen and yet have believed" (John 20:29). That same faith that must believe that God is, must also believe that He is a rewarder of those who seek Him. *Rewarder* is a noun, not a verb. God is *El Shaddai* and *Jehovah Jireh*. Our Father God does not just *do* abundance—He *is* abundance! He is our Father. How we see our Father determines what we will receive from Him.

God built within us a godly desire for honor and rewards. Honor and reward is what positions us for our next assignment. Rewards are not always monetary, but they always include honor. Honor normally opens the doors for greater opportunities and financial increase. Everyone is "hidden" for a certain season for godly reasons. It isn't wise to try to promote ourselves out of our "hidden season." That shows a basic lack of trust in God's ability and timing. We normally fight God more about the timing of our life rather than His ability to complete it. True humility is tested when God is doing more through us than others realize and He has the mute button pressed.

> "...*the man who kills Goliath the king will enrich with great riches, will give him his daughter, and give his father's house exemption from taxes in Israel'"* (1 Sam. 17:25 ESV).

David placed his life in danger, trusting that God would deliver him from Goliath. A greater battle would occur after Goliath was defeated. David wouldn't receive what he was promised. He would be robbed from all the promised rewards after a stunning God-given victory. We see no record of David receiving wealth from Saul. Presumably, Saul didn't think he should give a warrior's reward to a youth. David was a part of Jesse's family and had no personal property.

The daughter promised in marriage, Merab, was given away to another on his wedding day. It is interesting to note that Merab means—increase or manipulation. We must recognize that the enemy will try to manipulate situations when we reach our place of increase. We can't drop our guard after great victories that God determines for our increase—manipulation is always present, trying to steal our increase. Any spirit of unworthiness in us gives place for manipulation to steal our reward and promotion.

The enemy will always try to steal our rewards from victorious battles to discourage us from living on the front lines of faith. We are not ignorant of the enemy's devices. Stay in faith, David. The promise is still in front of you! Continue to seek Him. Don't let your vision drop because of what man is doing to you. Look at what God is doing in you and what He is doing for you, David. God will make up anything that man takes from us—if we keep our heart on Him.

Twenty-nine years prior to David fighting Goliath, Israel had chosen to have a king like all the nations around them. This transition had occurred at the end of Samuel's reign. As a result, over the years the children of Israel developed confidence for victory based on the size and strength of their armies. Israel was mesmerized by the system of power they had chosen and they had lost sight of Lord Sabbaoth. Without the *Lord Sabbaoth*, the Lord of the armies of God, Israel had been reduced to mere warriors—depending on their abilities alone. Only David could still see God, the warrior, in the midst of the intimidation of Goliath—who David trusted to fight with and through him.

David knew that a victory over the giant would move him closer to the prophecy that he received from Samuel. How could David fail in this battle? He had covenant with God and a promised future. He was not leaping off a cliff—he was stepping into his calling. The Chinese word for "crisis" is made from two symbols. The first symbol means "danger" and the second one means "opportunity." Our view of a crisis reveals how we truly see God and ourselves. Can we see the "God opportunity" in the crisis? Everyone can see the danger. Only those who can see the opportunity have the ability to step past the danger. Heroes and leaders are revealed in the midst of crisis and confusion. Live a bit more dangerous.

The Purpose of Fame

Several years ago, I started praying the following prayer: "Lord, make me as famous as I need to be to fulfill my purpose. Not one bit more or one bit less. Lord, bless me with all the finances I need to fulfill my total purpose, including blessing others. Not one cent more or one cent less." So much time would be wasted if the U.S. President was not well known. Everywhere he would go, he would be required to prove who he was before he could do anything. We are known by what we have done and it connects us to what we need to do. Being recognized is an essential key to fulfilling our destiny. The President of the United States has fewer keys than anyone working in the White House. His identity is his key. Our known identity will unlock and open doors for us as well. Others have keys to open doors that we can't, but they must know us and our purpose. *If we do not discover our purpose, it will never be known by others.* David perceived he was king.

When David killed Goliath, it positioned him in the heart of Israel to be a king. In the span of one day, David went from being an unknown minstrel to being seen as a powerful warrior in the hands of God. A good reputation and a well-known identity with proven gifts will enable us to move seamlessly through life with others so that God's greater plans can unfold perfectly. Greater revelation of the Father releases a greater move of His presence and power. God is investing in our name, to make His name known. We are sons that resemble, represent, and honor our Father.

In baseball, a team needs athletes who are known for greatness in certain strategic positions to win the World Series. While each player must be able to catch and throw the ball, other specific skills are required for greatness in each position. With the nine greatest pitchers in baseball on the field for one team, winning several games would be possible, but never a World Series. Which pitcher could field the hard hit balls and slam a home run? Very few of the world's greatest pitchers!

Michael Jordan wasn't the greatest athlete of his era—he was the greatest basketball player. He loved baseball, so he switched sports. Even though he trained intensely, he struggled to be a minor league baseball player. He returned to basketball and to his destiny. If he would have pursued baseball instead of basketball, no one would know his name today. We should stick with the gifts, talents, or calling that God has given us. A gift that is part of our calling is responsive to training and use. Playing baseball for a season helped Michael Jordan understand his greatest gift with more clarity. He returned to basketball, and the Bulls went on to win another "three-peat."

Leaders have told me that they aren't sure they're in the right area of ministry. A struggling pastor wonders if they should be a teacher at a Bible college. A full-time traveling minister no longer enjoys the success or fulfillment that they did several years ago. They believe for greater things, but those things aren't happening and they are struggling financially. God will also test us with hard times, but He also can signal a "season shift" through limited or no success. If there has been a personal moral failure or stronghold that is ruling in our lives, it can steal or limit the anointing and block needed victories that God has held in the heavens until we breakthrough. God cares more about us than our ministry. He is willing to allow us to fail until He has our heart. A spiritual father is very helpful in discerning these difficult seasons.

Many gifts are required to be a successful leader. That fact alone can bury our greatest gift among our many gifts especially as we grow over time and our purpose expands. Great leaders enjoy an unusual level of success because they are multi-gifted, but that doesn't necessarily mean that they clearly see their greatest gift. Some of our greatest gifts tend to operate naturally because God has built them into us. We can be oblivious to the fact that one gift has more impact than the others because it is a part of everything we do. The uniqueness of our gift makes us special in a room full of people who have the exact same gift. We are not an echo on God's earth. One of His greatest joys is to find someone on earth who will represent Him and speak His words from their unique created identity.

I was counseling a couple who had a very troubled marriage. The husband, who initially was forced to come for counseling, later shared about the aspect of the ministry that was the most life changing for him. It was the prayers that I had him repeat after me. He repeated words to his wife concerning repentance, recommitment and restoration. He was a minister that had lost his way. As I gave him the words to speak—words which he could not find in that dark time—it brought light to him and life to his wife. I didn't see it as the most important key, even though I sensed a strong anointing on it. I had used that technique before with others, but under-valued it until he explained it from his perspective.

We are not always fully aware how powerfully God is working through us in specific situations. As we grow more aware of how God works through us, we'll be able to partner with Him more effectively and efficiently. We should become an expert in our strengths—or should I say His strength working in us. We can see the top of a mountain from a distance. After several hours of climbing the mountain, we think we have almost reached the top until getting to that peak that reveals the next "top." This can happen several times to an inexperienced mountain climber. When we actually reach the pinnacle, we gain an incredible view connected to our purpose. At the top of our "God" mountain we will see Him, ourselves, and our destiny from His view. This will release a season of convergence that will accelerate our purpose.

Chapter Five

THE GARDEN OF IDENTITY

Satan created the first identity crisis for mankind in the Garden of Eden. Satan cast shadows on God's relationship to Adam and Eve and His integrity saying that God was withholding knowledge from Adam and Eve that would make them like Him. The first attack was against God's identity — His identity as their Father. The next attack was against the identity of Adam and Eve. Satan implied that Father God had made them inferior when they were already made in His image and likeness. Satan knew he could steal their identity if he could first create doubt concerning the Father's love for them and His truthfulness to them.

Adam and Eve "bit" the lying accusations the enemy used to steal their identity. They believed they were inferior as fear of who they were and pride of who they could make themselves entered into their hearts — causing them to rebel. *Their identity was lost as they reached for the knowledge of man and not the life of the Father.* Satan is predictably boring in his most effective attacks against us. He accuses God to us and then he tells us there is something wrong with us. If we believe our Father God is wrong, how can we, His sons and daughters, be right?

Satan's fall was an identity crisis generated by his pride and rebellion. When he lost his identity, he lost his assignment. His identity changed from Lucifer, the light-bringing morning star archangel, to Satan—the father of lies and darkness. Satan's attitude of pride that caused him to lose his place in God's kingdom is his most effective attack against our calling. *Insecurity makes us vulnerable to pride.* Satan's strategy is to steal our identity in order to stop our assignments. Why? Our assignments will crush him and set people free that are presently held by his darkness. The enemy invades our identity with thoughts of inferiority at strategic transitions to cause us to disqualify ourselves for what God has already chosen us to do!

The journey of our lives is to gain back our identity through Jesus, the last Adam. God is restoring in us that which the first Adam lost. After the fall, Adam and Eve covered themselves to hide from each other—then they both *hid together* from God. This is a picture of the identity crises that now tries to dominate earth. The enemy has blocked our relationship with Father God and with people. We must have our identity restored to fully engage Father God and mankind or we will never shift the earth.

Then the eyes of both of them were opened, and they knew that they were naked; and they sewed fig leaves together and made themselves coverings. And they heard the sound of the LORD God walking in the garden in the cool of the day, and Adam and his wife hid themselves from the presence of the LORD God among the trees of the garden. Then the LORD God called to Adam and said to him, "Where are you?" So he said, "I heard Your voice in the garden, and I was afraid because I was naked; and I hid myself." And He said, "Who told you that you were naked?" (Genesis 3:7-11 NKJV).

Adam and Eve had clothed themselves with fig leaves that they had sown together, yet they referred to themselves as naked when responding to God from their hiding place. We cannot cover our own nakedness with the work of our hands, only the Father's love can cover us. The intimate relationship they enjoyed with God was shattered by their shame and fear. Man is always trying to cover his shame, while God is offering us His love and His honor through Jesus.

God asked Adam a very important question; "Who told you that?" It is very important to realize that Satan spoke through the serpent. The enemy must find various people to speak through to steal your identity. Actions can speak louder than words, so the adversary will also cause people to treat us in a devaluing manner. Children are usually confident and innocent in nature, until someone embarrasses them or speaks to them in a negative way. God is still asking us the same question to help us; "Who told you that? Would you please believe Me?"

If a police officer had his uniform, badge, gun and police car stolen, he could not operate as an officer in his area of jurisdiction. That which reveals and confirms his identity has been taken, even though headquarters will confirm that he is a police officer. Headquarters is confirming our identity, but we will never enter our *purpose with authority* until we are "wearing" the mantle of our identity. In the beginning, God mantled them in light, even as He is, and gave Adam and Eve dominion. The serpent talked them out of their identity—thus their dominion was lost and the glory of their Father that clothed them was reduced to shame. Jesus is speaking to us to restore our identity as sons and daughters of the Father. Jesus prayed that the glory He shared with the Father would be given back to us. The glory that clothed Adam and Eve is being restored to us in our relationship with our Father God.

The same enemy that destroyed the relationship between Adam and Eve—and them and God—is coming after we who are restored. While they were sinless, the serpent talked them out of their identity. They lost their authority and purpose in a pretty nice place as they agreed with Satan's thoughts! Our surroundings and circumstances never determine our future, our relationship with the Father and our identity do. As we know who we are to the Father—our identity and our destiny unfold. When we are living in our "garden of purpose" we can't expect Satan's undermining attacks to cease.

> *... the son of Enosh, the son of Seth, the son of **Adam**, the son of God (Luke 3:38 NASB).*

God gave Adam, *His son*, dominion in the Garden of Eden that He created. He chose to be a Father to Adam, who would rule the earth with this intimate robust relationship. God entrusted Adam. God designed Adam in His image and likeness to be a son who could please the Father. God formed the animals out of the dirt and then refused to name them. Then The Father brought the animals before Adam to see what he would name them. Normally whenever someone makes something, they name it. God wanted a unique relationship with us from the beginning. There are many things and situations that God will bring in front of us, waiting to see what we will name it—and what we name it, it shall be! Amazing! What will we name our nation, our church, our children, our job or our future? God is waiting to see what we will name it, just like Adam.

The greatest move of God is found back in the Garden of Eden. It is not about a perfect place with no troubles. It was a utopia filled with the presence of God with two deadly deceiving forces in it: the serpent and the Tree of the Knowledge of Good and Evil. These are things that should not be forgotten. God walked and talked with Adam and Eve daily in an intimate purposeful relationship. The serpent was also given a voice by God to talk with them as well. I would have never allowed it. Yet God desired to be surrounded by those who choose Him—don't all of us? He put us in a world of choices. Even the angels were given a window of choice.

Adam was made in the image and likeness of his Father—man was minted in the Father's identity. God took Eve out of Adam and asked them to operate as one—giving both of them dominion in the Garden. The Tree of Life was available, but not sought by them. The serpent was not after the Garden of Eden, *he was after Adam's and Eve's identity.*

"And He walks with me and He talks with me and He tells me I am His own. And the joy we share as we tarry there, no other has ever known." That hymn has great revelation. There is a joy we share in His presence that empowers us for His Kingdom. When we live the words of that famous song, we will change and things around us start changing.

We are to live from His presence and bring Him glory as we walk in dominion on the earth. This dominion does not control other people, but it influences and directs people to make quality decisions that affect the earth. That dominion is demonstrated and reinforced by self-control. If we are out of control of our earthen vessel how can we have dominion in the earth? We can change the world by changing someone's world. As we yield our life on this earth to honor Him, it will influence those around us to look toward God. This is a mountaintop view that has practical applications for believers in every walk of life. We must never allow the enemy to underestimate the importance of our life.

God has chosen unique gardens in different seasons of our lives to give us opportunity to flourish. The Garden of Gethsemane was a garden of adversity and commitment that preceded Jesus' greatest victory. A captured Israelite servant girl told Naaman that her God could heal him if he would go to the man of God. She did not allow her limited position in life and the garden of oppression that she had not chosen to steal the greatness that God put inside of her to believe for miracles—even if it was for her oppressor. She had more faith than the King of Israel. After Naaman was healed, she received a blessing. We know he desired to bless Elisha and even gave gifts to Gehazi—after Elisha refused them. She might receive the greatest reward in heaven for that miracle. You may not have chosen your garden, but you can decide what happens in it.

Fathers of faith create *gardens* where identity of others can be revealed and flourish. We must not be afraid to help others develop their greatness by seeding our greatness into their lives. Wherever we have fruit, our purpose and destiny is revealed. Every tree is known by its fruit, not its bark. "So then, you will know them by their fruits." (Matt. 7:20, NASB) If an apple tree grows bananas, it will be known as a banana tree even though it has apple tree bark! Some people have more bark than fruit. It is powerful when people have their voice and fruit aligned. That is the way God designed His world. In our fruit are the seeds that will help others grow the same fruit. Seedtime and harvest will never end—it is true in people as well as crops.

We must understand the function of our specific gifts that God has entrusted to us before we can raise up others. As we teach and impart it to others to reproduce it in them, the Holy Spirit releases a greater revelation and authority to us. What we did intuitively from our God-given gifts and acquired wisdom becomes clearer to us as we teach it. Those learning can stand on our shoulders of knowledge, but they will still have to develop the heart and the anointing that it takes to live in that knowledge. Any teaching that we receive from others, just like natural food, must be eaten, digested, and integrated before it becomes part of our life. The Holy Spirit will help us break it down into practical teachings and principles that will bring success to those who apply them.

Looking from afar, Jesus expected there to be figs on that fig tree (Matt. 21). When people look at us from a distance, what kind of fruit do they expect? How did God design us? What fruit does Jesus desire from our tree? He perfectly designed each of us to bear unique fruit for His kingdom.

The scripture says that the eyes of the Lord are searching throughout the earth to find someone whose heart is loyal that He may show Himself strong on their behalf. (2 Chron. 16:9) Father God made each of us special and important—that's why there are endless possibilities of whom He could choose. It is a heart issue, not a talent requirement. Now He is simply searching for someone who believes what He can do and that He can do it through them. He needs us to agree with Him concerning our identity so that He can freely move through us. His identity is revealed in the scriptures and through the life of Christ—and through each of our lives. He desires to show Himself strong through us. He would like to use each of us. He is still sowing seed into the hearts of men in every generation, expecting a great harvest.

Clarifying Your Gift

If you want to clarify your gift and purpose here is one method that could prove helpful. Pick five to twelve people for a simple survey. All of these people should have a current relationship with you. Someone who has only known you for a short time could also offer an interesting perspective. Different types of relationships could speak to different areas and giftings, but they still will overlap. The following types of people would be good to ask:

- Father/Mother
- Close Friends. (Your Spouse/Uncle/Aunt/Brother/Sister/Cousin)
- People who work with you. (Supervisors/Peers/Subordinates)
- People who have been influenced by you.

Ask them these three questions:

1. What do you see as my greatest gift/strength? (top three)

2. What has been my greatest influence or inspiration in your life?

3. What story, experience or conversation comes to mind when you think of these things?

People's stories can often contain elements that they may not recognize, but which become clearer as you study the remarks made by others, as well as your own insight into your journey.

When you ask others for their input, write the questions down or send an email. This allows the participants to process the material and communicate their answers through writing. It will require greater reflection on their parts, and be more helpful to you as you gather the data. Compare their answers.

Now ask God these same questions in a quiet time after coming before Him in worship. Write at least three major aspects of Him that you adore. Be sure to write down your thoughts as you are in His presence. His quiet voice is often in our thoughts.

1. "Father God, what is my greatest/gift strength You have given me?" (top three)

2. "Father God, what is my greatest influence or inspiration to others?"

3. "Father God, remind me of key events and conversations that confirm my gifts and purpose."

Think of the major challenges and victories in your life. What was He building and maturing in your identity for your destiny?

List your dreams and desires for your future.

1. Expect your dream list to be your future.
2. Start making plans to each point in your list.
3. Prioritize the importance of each dream.
4. Put them in order according to the journey you are traveling.
5. Declare them to a friend.

Complete this task *before* you receive or review feedback from others. Consider them again after receiving feedback from others. This process is strategic to fulfilling your destiny. Most of us do it naturally as we gather information from many sources and events. Being intentional is helpful, providing greater insight.

Now, make a list of three qualities that you admire in other people. Do you see those qualities in yourself? What qualities do you need to add or strengthen to be more effective in your greater gifts? Ask the Lord. Sometimes our greatest natural gifts never come to fullness because of other supporting qualities that are never developed through discipline. If our strength is talking, listening is our natural weakness. If spontaneity is our greatest strength, planning is our natural weakness. If planning is our greatest gift, missing unexpected opportunities would be our natural weakness. We need to continue to sharpen our greatest gift, but strengthen natural weakness needed to aid your greatest gift.

Our personal abilities—mental, spiritual, and physical—are the core of who God made us. We are God's genius. The gifts of God flow in believers by the Holy Spirit. The Holy Spirit rests in our spirit and activates our abilities. Personal abilities can be uncovered, nurtured, or even created in our journey with God. The gifts of the Holy Spirit are God's abilities—the raw power of God—on loan from heaven to use on earth. The fruit of the Spirit is the nature and character of God. The gifts and the fruit of the Spirit are designed to flow through every believer. When we understand who we are and what our purpose is, we become more effective in our destiny.

How we train and use our natural and spiritual gifts will determine the level of authority God will grant us. There are some gifts hidden from our eyes until we move into that which we have already been entrusted. Unfaithful servants can never receive their full God-given destiny. To the faithful servants, He gives more. To the unfaithful, He takes away what He gave. Faithfulness is just a decision away. When we turn our decision into faithful action, what was removed—is restored to us. We must use what He has given us, before He will give us more. If we do not highly value the gifts God has given us, we will never make an impact with them.

Praise Him for them! Study them in the scriptures. Observe them in operation in others. Receive greater understanding and anointing from the teaching of others who move in those callings and gifts. We must hunger for God to use our lives for His glory. *Here am I. Send me!*

God spoke to me clearly years ago. He said, "If you do not increase, you cannot participate in what I have planned for you in this coming season. If you would see yourself the way I do, we could go places." The Lord had my full attention. Those words echoed through my mind and spirit.

He had prepared my destiny for me. It was reserved for me. It was my time. It was greater than anything I had previously done. Yet according to His words, I wasn't ready to participate in it. My lack of agreement with Him concerning my identity was the main blockage. That drove me deeper into prayer quickly. Revelation came: First, get rid of every negative thing that brings decrease and limitations to my identity, destiny, anointing, purpose, and abilities. I broke several mindsets that were lies that had become my expectation. My identity had been twisted by my agreement with these negative expectations. Negative expectations block the anointing. Lies are sometimes facts masquerading as truth. We must dismantle those lies to walk in the fullness of our destiny. I came across the following scripture which helped me better understand the issue.

"Little by little I will drive them out before you, until you have increased enough to take possession of the land" (Exod. 23:30, NIV).

Israel had to increase to receive what God had already promised. To increase, we must see ourselves through God's eyes. We will obtain revelation as we walk forward with Him as He drives them out before us. We will not see it sitting in the stands observing, it's time to take the field. A professional athlete increases his skills while playing against the best. This is not a practice run, this is our life.

God brought truth to certain life expectations I had in front of me. He said, "If you would see yourself the way I do, we could go places." I realized that I didn't agree with God about myself! I was surprised! I thought my block was probably rooted in my lack of faith in Him. It wasn't. It was my lack of faith in me. It was the mindsets that the enemy had embedded in my identity through disappointing experiences. God was driving them out in front of me, little by little.

To fulfill your "God destiny" you must see yourself the way your Father sees you. Your destiny was designed to draw you into a deeper encounter with your Father. Many Christians need an identity realignment. Your identity is revealed as you see aspects of your Father God with greater clarity. If you do not see Him correctly or more fully, you will never perceive who He has made you. The Father has invested part of His identity in each of His sons and daughters. We are made in

His image so that we have the ability to carry "our part" of who He is. Our purpose is found in our identity. True sons reveal the Father. The Father's joy is to reveal His sons and daughters.

What was true in the last season could be a lie in the next season. Our past can distort our new assignments and new identity, limiting our new season if the purpose of our past is not properly related to the future. David's responsibility was to watch Jesse's sheep as a youth. He could not leave the sheep as soon as Samuel anointed him to be the next king of Israel. After David was crowned king of Israel, it would have been foolish ignorance and rebellion to his call to start watching Jesse's sheep again.

Would we let a homeless thief live in our house if we had an empty bedroom because he has a need? No! Once he's inside our house, he has access to everything. It will cost us more to have a lie live in our mind than a thief to live in our house. A thief can steal our possessions, but a lie will steal our destiny. Ask Jesus to expose the lies you believe about yourself. It is the most effective plan the enemy has to hold us back from our destiny. Many Christians have allowed the thief to live in their minds too long and they are often hidden under insecurities. We cannot kick out the thief until we find him. Satan knows the best thief is the invisible and undiscovered thief. If we can't see him, we can't stop him. When we expose him, his activity and damage is stopped. What hurt is he hiding behind or beneath? A thief knows how and where to hide. What disappointment has he used to downgrade our expectations? Let's uncover the thief and get our "stuff" back.

Overcoming Opinions and Emotions

*When Eliab, David's oldest brother, heard him speaking with the men, he **burned with anger** at him and asked, "Why have you come down here? And with whom did you leave those few sheep in the desert? I know how conceited you are and how wicked your heart is; you came down only to watch the battle." (1 Sam. 17:28 NIV)*

David was publicly and hurtfully judged by his older brother, Eliab, in front of the army of Israel on the day of battle. Eliab was a seasoned warrior who stood head and shoulders above David and those around him. The intimidation factor was off the chart. Naturally, David would have looked up to his oldest brother. The enemy used Eliab to unseat David's heart and faith at a very strategic moment in David's development. Eliab judged David as having a wicked heart when actually it was his heart that was impure. David lived in Father God's heart so he was not swayed by the harsh judgments of his brother. The enemy was baiting David to judge his brother in anger.

David did not allow those words to move him out of God's presence. If David had responded in bitterness, Goliath would have won! "Goliath battles" always produce an identity shift, so few or none will see you capable of handling Goliath before the battle. Your Father who spoke your identity into your heart years ago is now ready to reveal it. David could not change Eliab's mind, nor was it his assignment. After Eliab saw Goliath defeated, his view of Samuel's choice shifted.

The voice of an "older brother" will often put us down just before we face Goliath. Each believer must overcome family issues to enter the fullness of their call. God wants a higher position in our heart than our family, yet He wants us to love them through it all. If we can defeat that negativity while walking in love, we will have the anointing to defeat Goliath. We can't let doubt and negative thoughts take us out of our God opportunity. We must learn to handle negative words before we can handle a Goliath. David wasn't side-tracked into defending himself with his brother, but he kept his focus on his opportunity.

David not only had to battle the devaluing words, but also the anger that was *burning* inside of Eliab. Emotional attacks can be more difficult to navigate and repel than the negative words that are spoken. Anger and accusations are released by the enemy through others attempting to break down our love and peace to steal our faith. The goal of the enemy is to cause us to respond back in the same spirit of accusation so that he can control, defeat or stop us. When we step out of our Father God's emotions into the enemy's emotions that are flowing through the antagonistic person, we are easily defeated. The peace of God is required to crush Satan under our feet.

Peace is an *emotion* that flows from the *thoughts* of Christ concerning the problem. Emotional attacks always precede our Goliath victory. Negative emotions leave when we think differently. They might leave temporarily with a mood swing, but they can only be eradicated when we chose to think the truth. Truth dismantles the lies that produce the negative emotions. If we use our mind to control the negative emotions instead of changing our thoughts, it is very draining and an impossible mission. It is backwards living.

One of the reasons emotions were given to us by God is to add inspiration to truth. It is a motivator and a finishing factor. Our emotions strengthen our belief. Truth expressed with corresponding emotions, convey truth in a convincing way. When a person speaks facts that are true with inappropriate emotions, we instinctively know that something is wrong. If someone whispers to us that our house is on fire, we will not believe them.

Our window of opportunity is connected to our call, anointing, and purpose. That window is a key assignment to elevate us into our destiny. It requires "now" faith and "now" action. Heaven has many "revolving doors" of opportunity, but major strategic doors of opportunity must be apprehended within the time frames of heaven. Goliath opportunities are rare, but included in each person's life. "Davids" will meet the challenge confidently because they battled the lion and the bear when few or none were watching. Our private victories are the foundation of our public victories. The sense of destiny will propel us through our windows of opportunity.

> *"David said to Saul, 'Let no one lose heart on account*
> *of this Philistine; your servant will go and fight him.*
> *'Saul replied, 'You are not able to go out against this*
> *Philistine and fight him; you are only a young man,*
> *and he has been a warrior from his youth'"* (1 Sam.
> *17:32–33, NIV).*

David was now standing before Saul, the greatest warrior in Israel. David was not even born when Saul became king. Saul had decades of victories under his belt. David was only seventeen years old and King Saul was fifty nine years old. Saul told David that he wasn't able to go out against the Philistine. David didn't become defensive or angry. Insecurity has a defensive attitude and David wasn't. David could have pointed out to King Saul that it was his harp and singing that drove the tormenting spirits from the king. David could have informed King Saul that God had already chosen him years ago to be the next king through Samuel. David refused to lift himself above Saul, but he rose to the occasion.

> *But David said to Saul, "Your servant used to keep*
> *his father's sheep, and when a lion or a bear came*
> *and took a lamb out of the flock, I went out after it*
> *and struck it, and delivered the lamb from its mouth;*

and when it arose against me, I caught it by its beard, and struck and killed it. Your servant has killed both lion and bear; and this uncircumcised Philistine will be like one of them, seeing he has defied the armies of the living God." Moreover David said, "The Lord, who delivered me from the paw of the lion and from the paw of the bear, He will deliver me from the hand of this Philistine." And Saul said to David, "Go, and the Lord be with you!" (1 Sam. 17:34–37, NKJV)

David gave King Saul a reason to allow him to fight Goliath. David spoke of his previous impressive victories that any man would respect. We should always be ready to give any man a reason for the hope that lies within us as well as anything God has called us to do. David wasn't cornered into a fight by those wild animals, he initiated the fight. He pursued the lion and the bear to save a lamb. He displayed incredible courage, taking the lamb from a lion and the bear. If you remove lunch from a lion's mouth, you are next on his menu. When the lion rose up to kill David, he seized it by its hair and struck it down. There was no sling used to kill that lion.

David, like Jesus, took the lamb out of the lion's mouth and placed himself in the face of death, believing that God would deliver him. David had an incredible faith based in an incredible relationship. It was not a foolish test with the enemy, but a rescue mission based in the heart of God. David knew God delivered him from the lion and the bear. He knew that God would deliver him from the hand of the Philistine. David was not counting on his sling proficiency, but rather his Deliverer. David was not afraid to position himself in a place of danger for the purposes of heaven.

When someone starts talking down to you, the enemy is attempting to steal your confidence and identity. David did not allow his brother, King Saul or Goliath to provoke him to anger. Guard your destiny with truth, not anger. There are negative words that you can ignore without correction, but there are other negative words that carry weight in the spirit. They will alter you, your assignment or the atmosphere around you if you do not openly reject it. Smile and firmly say, "I do not receive that." Then walk away. You are not trying to change their mind, you are guarding yours. Like David, make good your escape when they try to pin you to the wall.

The Value of a Son

David's victories not only demonstrate his great faith, but also the very intimate relationship that David had with God. David also understood the value that he had before his Father God. God was overinvested in David and He protects His investments. Father God is overinvested in us too, through Jesus Christ, and the great price He paid for our salvation.

Several years ago I had a dream in which I saw Jesus walking toward me. He was coming in the spirit of Elijah— turning the hearts of the children to the Father. I heard Him say, "The simple gospel is this; the Father sent a Son to restore a son back to the Father."

The price of art is determined by the bids of interested buyers, with consideration given for the unique talent of the artist that produced it and limited production. Jesus, God's only Son, paid the price to purchase and restore us to the Father who made us in His image and likeness. It takes a Son to buy a son. Throughout time and eternity God will never create a duplicate of you. In heaven, God will give you a new name. No one else will have that name in all of heaven. When He calls your new name with billions of saints surrounding you, no one will turn their head but you.

A Rolex and a Timex are both watches, but their value is worlds apart. It would be foolish to pay tens of thousands of dollars for a Timex watch. Father God is not foolish. He paid the proper and fitting price to restore you back to Himself. People expect to pay tens of thousands of dollars for a Rolex. Value is connected to the manufacturer. You are a Rolex, not a Timex. An angel could not have paid the price for us. It took Jesus, His Son. Remember, we were created in His image and likeness so it took Him to restore us. *It took His Son to restore a son.*

David's stories and faith changed Saul's mind. King Saul actually blessed David to fight Goliath before he offered David his armor. David was anointed to kill Goliath, but it was not in his sphere of authority. That sphere of authority belonged to King Saul. He gave David his permission and blessing to fight Goliath. This shouldn't be overlooked. David was actually authorized to face Goliath by King Saul. David learned how to receive authority from God and man. If David had been offended by Saul's initial comments and had just run out to fight Goliath, the results wouldn't have been the same, even if he had won. Remember, Saul won his first battle where he lost it all.

It wasn't just David's faith alone that won the battle. He also connected to the authority that God placed over and in his life. God elected to keep Saul as king of Israel to defeat the Philistines, even though God rejected him for the greater generational blessings. David was required by God to honor Saul, knowing that God had rejected Saul. All of us struggle to honor people that do not support, agree or love us. That is one of the major requirements to be a true "David." It's not about what they did. Will we use it as an excuse or reason to change what God wants us to do? Who do we live before? That's great that we live before God. Let's keep our responses pleasing to Him and not ourselves. The faint hearted and the uncommitted need not apply for leadership.

Offenses always come before promotions in order to block us from receiving heaven's best. The enemy will always try to block the new level of authority that God is about to release to us. The enemy is trying to transform those offenses into hurt, then anger and ultimately rebellion. That would lessen or remove the God's anointing from our lives and accompanying assignments. Don't fall for the schemes of Satan.

God is watching how we handle offense. Offensive situations are used as qualifying tests preceding our promotions. We tend to judge others by what they do, but we judge ourselves by our intentions. We tell ourselves that others failed, while assuring ourselves that we meant well. If we can't handle the offense, we won't be able to handle the new level of authority and responsibility. What we know does not determine what we do. Knowledge is very powerful, but it is not always the determining factor. Our heart is. Do we invite God into the hurtful situations before we respond? Do we ask Him to reveal the cause of the anger that we feel rising within us? Whenever we lose it emotionally and spiritually, there is a deeper reason than simply the current events. God is using a present situation to uproot an attitude that was created in our past. He is challenging us to mature by exposing ungodly attitudes or unhealed hurts. Only tested and approved vessels, that continually yield to His dealings, shall carry the glory long-term.

Satan knows that a well-placed offense is one of the most effective methods of getting us out of God's timing, anointing and wisdom. Carnal anger produces ungodly responses that will steal, limit, or block our ability to step into our new season. If we can only see what others have done wrong, the enemy has rendered our discernment ineffective through self-righteousness. Our repentance for our faults, no matter how small they are in comparison to what was done to us, coupled with our forgiveness released to them, will reset our spirit and mind for another anointed opportunity.

Revelation can lead to deception if we center on what we know and not who we know. Self- importance and pride must be constantly resisted and rooted out at the edge of the ocean of revelation. He lifts us up as we humble ourselves. We cannot allow what we know and have experienced to lift us up; it is the same in nature as eating from the tree of the knowledge of good and evil. Lucifer was the most exalted archangel in heaven, closest to the throne. It went to his head and he lost it all. Satan battles revelation and anointing with pride, not lies. Pride contains deception that births error. Humility is not seeing ourselves low, but rather seeing Him so high that there is never any competition. Humility is the required companion to revelation.

Confidence in Your Window of Opportunity

We must remember David's station in life—he was a shepherd of his father's flock and the king's minstrel and armor bearer. He was not unfamiliar with the king, but he was not full-time in the palace by any stretch of the imagination. Taking care of the sheep would have required much of David's time. He was only needed during the infrequent times King Saul was tormented. David was in the midst of an identity stretch. David was seventeen years old standing in front of the king of Israel who was fifty-nine years old.

Saul's armor did not fit David since he was head and shoulders above him.

Stepping from the fields of Jesse to the courts of King Saul was a huge step. There was nothing that King Saul and David had in common. David could not use friendship to build a bridge with King Saul. King Saul would enter into times of torment where he needed David to calm his spirit as a minstrel. David was playing the harp for King Saul, but he was not there to strike up conversations with the king.

King Saul had twenty-nine years of military leadership as king of Israel, defeating the enemy time and time again. David is presenting himself to King Saul for his first military encounter of his life. Goliath challenged Israel with a one-on-one ultimate warrior fight unto death, with each nation bound to becoming servants of the victor's people. David is not only risking his life, but the outcome will determine the future of Israel. The warriors of Israel were in fear of Goliath and shocked as they saw David running towards him. Their fear was probably the only thing that kept the warriors of Israel from tackling David to increase their chances of victory by choosing someone older, stronger and more experienced to represent them in this winner-take-all fight-unto-death-match.

As soon as the warriors heard David address Goliath, they recognized his confidence and faith for victory. All Israel felt a shift in the atmosphere as David declared the victory of God in his fight. David was also in the face of Goliath, calling the victory in the first round, like many great fighters do. David's words flowed from his faith and his desire to honor the name of the Lord—and the Lord gave him the exact words he needed to win that battle. Sharp focus and purpose release a natural flow of words through our heart—from the heart of God.

David was confident that what God had done for him—He would do again. David won the right to fight the battle God had chosen for him. God's presence was deeply embedded into David's heart at such a young age. David responded with passionate worship towards God and His promises. It unlocked the greatness He created in David. When David was called into King Saul's presence, he was not presumptuous or nervous. Until we can confidently present ourselves before others who have greater authority, we will never be given the opportunity to enter our dream.

Joseph also knew how to present himself at his limited window of opportunity to enter his God dream. Joseph had been in prison for over two years. Pharaoh sent for Joseph, and he was quickly brought from the dungeon. When he was cleaned up with a fresh change of clothes, he came before Pharaoh. Joseph responded in such a level of confidence before Pharaoh that we almost miss it as he gives God credit. "I cannot do it," Joseph replied to Pharaoh, "but God will give Pharaoh the answer he desires." Joseph was confident in God and himself before Pharaoh. Joseph knew his "God gift" would work. Our gift will make room for us—especially in hard times and difficult situations.

Joseph did not stop speaking after interpreting both dreams, because Pharaoh may not have asked him to speak again. He did not want his past two years to become his permanent future! He must have felt an unusual presence of the Lord and self-awareness as he interpreted Pharaoh's *two dreams*, reminding him of the *two dreams* that God gave him as a young boy. Joseph made the most of his brief window of opportunity in a concise strategic way. Joseph had just finished doing what no wise man in the kingdom could do. "And now let Pharaoh look for a discerning and wise man and put him in charge of the land of Egypt." He did not stop there. Joseph laid out the plan for the next fourteen years that would save Egypt and increase its wealth.

Joseph was brought out of prison because he could interpret dreams. He stayed out of prison because he had a practical plan to deal with the impending national crisis. Joseph was learning how to run a nation while overseeing the prison—even while a prisoner. When we do the exceptional in the hard times, it will be impossible for the enemy to stop us from our God dream. Joseph did not try to plead his case of injustice before the man who could free him—that would have been a natural request of any prisoner. Joseph was not a prisoner—he was a dreamer. Joseph carried the dream in the prison. Therefore he related his opportunity to his dream, not the problem at hand. Our greatest opportunities are found in our most difficult situations. Joseph saw himself as a leader and he walked with confidence—just like David.

David and Joseph had to like who they were to survive the rejection they each faced. They agreed with God above and beyond their circumstances. We are told in scriptures that we must "love our neighbor as ourselves." If we love ourselves, our neighbor will have a better life. We are not talking about self-obsessions, but godly love. Love creates a boldness that empowers leadership where numerous quick decisions are required to succeed. If we are comfortable in our own skin, it will allow us live above intimidation. Intimidation is one of the enemy's great weapons. If we reject our vessel, we have rejected our mission. We must receive who God has made us, before we can step forward in the greatness the Father has given us.

Prayer: "Father, I receive that You have made me in Your image and likeness. Reveal my identity to me so that I can walk with You and fulfill my purpose in my generation. Reveal to me Lord any thoughts I have about myself with which You do not agree. I receive every good thought You have about me. I rejoice in You, who so wonderfully created me. I choose to passionately pursue You with all of my heart. Father God, You love me the best, so I expect and receive heaven's best."

Chapter Six

THE BATTLE OF WORDS

David said to the Philistine, "You come against me with sword and spear and javelin, but I come against you in the name of the Lord Almighty, the God of the armies of Israel, whom you have defied. This day the Lord will deliver you into my hands, and I'll strike you down and cut off your head. This very day I will give the carcasses of the Philistine army to the birds and the wild animals, and the whole world will know that there is a God in Israel. All those gathered here will know that it is not by sword or spear that the Lord saves; for the battle is the Lord's, and he will give all of you into our hands." (1 Sam. 17:45–47, NIV)

As David faced Goliath, he brought attention to the giant's weapons that Israel feared. David implied that he would use Goliath's own sword to cut off Goliath's head since he had none. David had prophetic insight that what the enemy was using to intimidate Israel, should be used to finish the battle. David had to counter the negative prophetic words that Goliath released over him and into the atmosphere before he ran toward him. When we decree God's word it shifts the atmosphere, pushing back demonic forces and inviting the angelic forces of heaven into the situation. David countered each point that Goliath shouted with his descriptive decree. We must win the battle of words before we engage the enemy in the battle. We must decree the outcome before the start of the fight. God declares the end from the beginning. Talk like your Father.

David realized Israel and the Philistines had forgotten that there was a God in Israel. David was well trained with a sling, but God was the one who landed the stone. David broke the spirit of unbelief and fear released through Goliath as he decreed the victory of the Lord. He refocused the entire army of Israel on the Lord. David went from addressing Goliath to putting the whole army of the Philistines on notice that they were next on the list to be defeated. David saw the victory beyond Goliath before he defeated Goliath. He literally was instilling seeds of faith against the enemies' lies, positioning Israel's army for breakthrough as soon as they saw his first words come to pass—Goliath defeated.

They did not believe David could back up what he said until he accomplished it. When Goliath dropped, Israel arose in faith and the Philistines fled in fear. The fear left Israel and moved to the Philistines. One significant victory can shift the expectations on both sides of the issue.

Be a game changer! Notice the last several words that David said: "For the battle is the Lord's, and He will give all of you into our hands." David painted all of Israel into the victory with his declaration. David created a place of faith to position the army of Israel to enter the battle. Our significant victory can get others, who are hiding in fear, back into the battle of faith.

Goliath means "shouter." Unbelief shouts at us. If insecurity was seated in David's heart, the shouts of unbelief would have connected to his fears and stopped David in his tracks. Goliath despised David. Goliath was enraged and insulted that a boy with a stick was chosen to fight him. Goliath shouted, "Am I a dog?" Pride and rage made Goliath an easy target. Goliath did not know he was facing the next king of Israel. David was immovable in his faith. He didn't respond to Goliath's insults because his identity was secure in his God. If we still need to prove who we are, we are still journeying to know who we are.

Unbelief always shouts the loudest before our greatest victories in God. The voice of unbelief will focus on us and our abilities in the most negative light possible. It will focus on the overwhelming size of the problem. It has a carnal view toward life that can be misinterpreted as sound advice. Unbelief has a voice of reason. It is very deceiving. Truth breaks lies. It takes revelation (truth anointed by the Holy Spirit) to dismantle deception (lies anointed by demonic spirits). Deception is based on lies, but yet it is different in nature. Lying is simply not telling the truth. Deception believes a lie is the truth. If we are deceived, we do not know it. If we are lying, we are aware that we are withholding truth.

Something shifted in David's focus as he made his last decrees to Goliath revealing his understanding of heaven's victories on earth. "This day the Lord will deliver you into my hands." David knew the hand of God would deliver him from Goliath, *but he also knew that God would give Goliath into his hands*. David saw God working through him. Christ dwelling in us is the hope of all glory and all victories we will experience on earth. We must see Him moving through us as well as helping us. David's identity was seamlessly connected to God. Our identity must lean into our Father's identity for Him to move through us. David emphasized God as being the source of victory over and over again. In the end he talked about himself and the army of Israel. To recover our identity, we will have to defeat the spirit of unbelief. Goliath is small compared to the enemy in our battle for identity.

If our greatest passion in life is for the Father, the provisions and the influential favor that the Father has for us will come to pass in God's timing. This does not mean that we will be the most famous person in the world, but in our world we will have all we need to fulfill God's destiny for our life. If we are only thankful to God because of what we receive, we are still not living as a son to the Father. We are now living as an orphan in the trap of insecurity, proving our worth by what we have instead of who we have. It is hard to slip back into an orphan's world of possessions, prestige and pride when our heart is fixed on Him. If our eyes gaze too long at our blessings, they can easily transform into idols. The enemy is always trying to capture God's best, so we must guard our heart. Greatness and wealth can never be a deciding factor for our identity. How much can we obtain and still retain the same spirit? At what level of greatness would we cave into becoming someone less in God's eyes?

David fell after he was established in his destiny as king of Israel, not during his journey to it. Success can be more difficult to navigate than the adversity faced in the journey toward it. David didn't pass one integrity test in the seductive atmosphere that always accompanies the privilege of power. Goliath was an easier battle than Bathsheba. Yet David understood something about God's heart that most people fail to comprehend. God wanted to forgive David more than David wanted to be forgiven. When confronted by Nathan, David went from self-righteous to repentant. David was truly a man after God's heart.

Think of the tests that we have passed. What did God forge in us? What knowledge or experience did we gain? Purposeful and effective progress is obtained through life's tests when we clearly understand what strengths God has developed in us. It is very important to retain the truth that was revealed. Understanding the test is just as important as passing the test. The goal of every test deals with understanding and ability. Store the knowledge and use the tools, strengths, and wisdom that God developed through that test.

Tests are not just designed to find out what we know, but they are also an invitation from heaven to learn His ways.

Many tests are given in open-book format, but the teacher will not talk to us until the test is over. We must remember what He told us and respond correctly. We are now being challenged to put our faith, knowledge and personal relationship with God into action in real-life situations. God is also like a coach helping us strategically, directing our thoughts and emotions. Reading the story about David and Goliath is not the same as running toward our Goliath. He's almost five times heavier than us, nearly twice as tall, and seven times stronger. If he so much as falls on us, we're dead!

If we are overconfident that we can handle a problem, our self-reliance becomes a greater problem in God's eyes. In such instances, we aren't asking God for wisdom, nor are we listening for Him to speak. We have become self-sufficient which is the fruit of pride and rebellion. Hearing God's voice is based upon our constant recognition of our need for Him and our personal invitation for Him to be a part of every moment of our life. Waiting on the Lord because He spoke, even when we know we can handle it, brings Him great pleasure. This is where king Saul lost it all.

Promotion Brings Conflict

When the victorious Israelite army was returning home after David had killed the Philistine, women

*from all the towns of Israel came out to meet King
Saul. They sang and danced for joy with tambourines
and cymbals. This was their song: "Saul has killed his
thousands, and David his ten thousands!" This made
Saul very angry. "What's this?" he said. "They credit
David with ten thousands and me with only thousands.
Next they'll be making him their king!" So from that
time on Saul kept a jealous eye on David. The very
next day a tormenting spirit from God overwhelmed
Saul, and he began to rave in his house like a madman.
David was playing the harp, as he did each day. But
Saul had a spear in his hand, and he suddenly hurled
it at David, intending to pin him to the wall. But David
escaped him twice. (1 Sam. 18:6–11, NLT)*

David was leading the armies of Israel into battle with
such tremendous success that the women sang songs of his
victories. There comes a time when God causes others to
celebrate our life and accomplishments before we reach our
"palace." Those celebrations will build us up to face the difficult season of rejection that is in front of us. It is a foretaste
of hope connected to the vision.

Ron and Teddy Sawka were unexpectedly celebrated at
a major leader's conference in Asia by the convener of that
gathering in front of 3,000 leaders, two weeks before my wife
and I arrived in Japan. I had heard from someone else how
deeply they were touched before they had a chance to share

that experience. I referred to the event in our conference to communicate and extend the honor that God brought to him and his wife, as most there had not yet heard about it. As we were deep in worship, I heard the Lord say to me, "Tell Ron these words; 'You must choose to live your life and ministry out of that celebration the Lord gave you. Refuse to live from anywhere else."

We must refuse to live from the hurts in our history. We must live from the Lord's celebrations over our lives. God releases celebrations in our life at strategic times to accelerate us into our next season. The enemy will attempt to use a victory or celebration to lure us into setting ourselves up as "king" prematurely instead of waiting on God's process. Celebrations over our lives will also ignite jealousy among the insecure. This jealousy will come after us, just as Saul came after David. It will help remove the Saul attitude in each of us and will qualify us for the throne as we respond correctly.

David formed a covenant relationship with Jonathan that endured beyond Jonathan's death. Jonathan was the heir to the throne, yet David related to him in such a way that Jonathan wanted David to be the next king instead of himself. This is one of the most improbable covenant relationships that ever existed on earth. David lived his life with such integrity that he wasn't offensive or obtrusive to Jonathan as he pursued his extraordinary call that automatically removed Jonathan's expected birthright.

Everyone is praying for us to increase until we surpass them. The root issue is not jealousy, but insecurity. Insecurity springs from a lack of identity. Jealousy and criticalness are the face and fruit of insecurity, but underneath it all is the lack of identity. Criticism is the hammer we use to drive someone down lower than us. People who prayed for you to succeed may not be happy with the sphere of promotion God gives you. Thankfulness and praise to God for His blessing to other sons and daughters preserves a right spirit and creates a safeguard from insecurity.

No matter how much God blesses anyone, no one can take from us or block what God has determined to give us. It will always be ours to receive, unless we become offended like the responsible brother in the story of the prodigal son. Even at the end of the story after the loving father told his hard-working son that everything that he had was always his, but he still *would not* ask his generous father for it. The well-behaved son again judged his merciful father for what he gave his irresponsible brother upon his return. This judgment blocked his ability to receive what the father desired to give him. It was literally set aside for the compliant son from the day his undisciplined brother left with his inheritance—the rest was all his, but now he *could not* ask for it. Self-righteous attitudes and judgments against our loving, merciful Father God will block our ability to receive our inheritance from Him.

David had been revealed as a mighty warrior and people were celebrating exuberantly. As the women made a song of comparisons, instead of glorifying God, the king became incredibly jealous and then suspicious. Saul chose his attitudes, but he did not choose his demon. Jealousy in one is often birthed in the middle of a celebration of another! That is normal. As the wise men were celebrating the one who was born king of Israel, King Herod struggled with insecurity until the slaughter of children became acceptable. Insecurity is never satisfied with what it has.

Jealously arises in friends and associates who are standing next to us when someone sings our praises too loudly. To counteract the jealousy that tends to arise in others, first we need to give thanks to God for what He has done through us—if it is in an appropriate setting. Also we should give honor to anyone who contributed to that accomplishment. We should look for opportunities to celebrate other people's accomplishments, especially those who seem jealous. It will diminish the spirit of jealousy as our words of honor help them feel more secure. We must also realize that the insecure cannot sustain a healthy attitude. We must guard our heart so we are not jealous when others enter their season of favor and honor. When we rejoice in someone else's victories we are crushing the insecurity the destroyer is trying to use to crush us. It purifies our hearts and qualifies us for greater things. It also indicates that our identity is established in Father God, not accomplishments, comparisons or the praises of man.

Our assignments are lost or limited without a healthy godly identity. Captivity never shattered Daniel's identity. His assignments remained the same through three different kingdoms. While Israel was being judged by God through other nations, Daniel judged and ruled in those very same nations. Our identity is a game changer. Our assignments hinge on it. When Samuel anointed Saul, he became a different man. It changed his heart. When Samuel anointed David, it never changed his heart. His heart was already right. It simply increased his anointing and vision.

When God mightily uses someone we perceive as less godly, less anointed, or less qualified, it rattles us to the core of our being. Especially if their success lies in the very area that God has promised to us! We might secretly say to God, "I would have never used them if I were you. What were you thinking? Didn't you see the weakness in their lives? I am more qualified. Why didn't you choose me instead of them?" Pride is knocking on our door. We are now standing at the edge of bitterness and disillusion. It is the first step into pride and rebellion. Remember, pride was the destructive force in Lucifer's fall, not character issues or lifestyle. Pride is the number-one weapon of the enemy. Pride brings an air of superiority that destroys true authority and value. Pride is a thirst that can never be quenched. It is accompanied by tormenting spirits that take the joy of out of life and all accomplishments.

There was a pastor—let's call him Steve—who headed a large church. Close friends joined that church and became leaders over time. At their first network conference meeting that I attended, I met Steve for the first time. It was announced that Steve and his wife had been chosen to minister to the pastors of the fledging network who needed marital counseling. I had been quite effective in marriage counseling, but totally new and unknown to the pastors in this network. During a brief encounter, I discerned that he had issues of pride that would trouble any marriage. I could easily see that he was tremendously gifted, but in need of a major personal adjustment as he was sinking in success. About a year later, I heard that he had run off with his secretary and quit the ministry. Soon afterward, my close friends who attended Steve's church divorced. Months later, their child said to me, "I used to believe God could do anything. Now my pastor is divorced and so are my parents. Where is God?" That last question was the enemy setting me up. Where was God in all of this? I had just judged Pastor Steve, but I did not realize that I had also judged God.

Many years later, I was at a pastor's conference that I didn't normally attend. Steve was sitting one row in front of me! Anger started boiling inside of me. Steve married his secretary and was back in ministry after working seven years outside of the church. God wasn't done with me. He turned up the heat. Several months later, an elder in my church told me their children had found a new church that was experiencing explosive growth. The church—in the same city where

Steve had pastored previously—already had eight assistant pastors and the pastor's name was Steve! The elder couldn't remember the last name of the head pastor, but when I said it, they said, "That's it. Isn't it wonderful to know that my children have found such a wonderful, growing church?" I smiled and replied, "Praise the Lord!" My plastic smile melted in my anger as I walked away!

These words came out of my heart! "God, that's not right!" God answered quickly and firmly, "You're not right." I was undeterred. "God, I've been faithful to my wife all these years. You owe me!" As soon as those words came out of my heart, I knew what I said was wrong. It surprised and shocked me to the core of my being. God responded with wisdom and mercy I shall never forget. He said, "My son, he knows that everything he has received from Me is by My mercy. I am a debtor to no man. If you think I owe you, I cannot bless you." I lifted my hands and said, "God, You don't owe me a thing. Just bless me. Just bless me. Just bless me." And He has!

Over the years in ministry I had heard so many different stories of pastors with great churches who lost it all. The main reason was failed marriages. Somehow I had made this the litmus test of God's blessings for my life and church. I also had unknowingly judged God for blessing other pastors that were not faithful in their marriages. This angry hidden thought had gained a place in my heart that set me against Father God. Judgments against our fathers are the number one destroyer of blessings.

Several weeks later, that same elder informed me that I had gotten Steve's last name wrong. I actually sat with the real "Steve" several years later and asked his forgiveness as we sat in his new church building that is larger than the one I was getting ready to build, with more people than I had. I was okay with that. I blessed Steve and he blessed me in my building project. I was actually okay with myself and okay with God. That is not as easy as it sounds. We have a Father who helps us. I love and adore Him.

Sons are blessed by their Father simply because they are His. The Father refuses to have employees run His Kingdom. His Kingdom belongs to His sons. If the Father paid us for what we have done, we would be reduced from a son to an employee. Employees receive wages, sons receive an inheritance. Which do we prefer? Inheritances take longer to acquire than wages, but they are superior! Wages are based on what we do. Inheritances are based on who we are. If the enemy steals or hides our identity from us, we cannot claim our inheritance. Our inheritance is waiting for us and will be given as soon as our identity is established. We will ask God with a greater expectation when we see Him as our Father who has named us in His will.

Self-righteousness is the most deceptive spirit. Our carnal flesh is collectively flakey and selfish. It can't be trusted in any of us. We need to be watchful and committed to making our flesh a burnt offering of worship. How? We must refuse to cater to our selfishness. We can't buy into all the reasons we give people when we're defending ourselves, especially if we're angry. We need to ask the Holy Spirit if He agrees with us. After we have done well, we still need to check in with the Father for additional insight. Did we treat them with ungodly anger? We should repent specifically to God and them, even if we know we have done less wrong! Self-righteous anger is an identity robber.

This is My beloved Son, in whom I am well pleased.
Hear Him! (Matt. 17:5, NKJV).

Of all the titles given to Jesus, "My Son" is the one the Father uses to point us in the right direction and the heart of their relationship. No matter the level of our abilities, anyone can live as a son. The Father wants us to clearly understand the type of relationship that He desires to build with us, as He builds through us. Jesus became the living example of a son. Jesus stood in the Father's presence. Jesus saw what the Father was seeing. Jesus said what the Father was saying. Jesus did what the Father was doing. Jesus operated as a son. His identity as the Son of God was the core of His being and power of His life and ministry. His identity unlocks ours.

Worthy to Receive

"Now the Israelites had been saying, 'Do you see how
this man keeps coming out? He comes out to defy

Israel. The king will give great wealth to the man who kills him. He will also give him his daughter in marriage and will exempt his family from taxes in Israel'" (*1 Sam. 17:25, NIV*).

Twice, David asked what would be done for the man who killed Goliath. The answer was public knowledge. If David didn't want the king's daughter in marriage, he could have quietly said something to Saul before or after facing Goliath. I am sure that David had seen Saul's daughters previously as he played his harp for the king. When David cut off Goliath's head and carried it to King Saul, it was to receive the publicly advertised reward that had been promised to any man who killed Goliath.

Saul said to David, "Here is my older daughter Merab. I will give her to you in marriage; only serve me bravely and fight the battles of the Lord." For Saul said to himself, "I will not raise a hand against him. Let the Philistines do that!" But David said to Saul, "Who am I, and what is my family or my clan in Israel, that I should become the king's son-in-law?" So when the time came for Merab, Saul's daughter, to be given to David, she was given in marriage to Adriel of Meholah. (1 Sam. 18:17–19)

Notice the negativity in the words David spoke to King Saul when he presented his daughter to David; "Who am I and what is my family?" It may have been an acceptable way to humbly speak when honored in Israel, but it will not allow us to access our inheritance from heaven. It opened the door for the enemy to steal David's honor, reward and blessing. Our negative words at the last minute can actually block a blessing that is already on the way. Negative words will come out of our mouth when the honor given to us is greater than our identity. We must learn to be comfortable with our successes within a healthy identity.

Our faith can obtain honor that our identity cannot contain. How can this be? Our faith believes what God can do during special moments and our identity concludes what He can do through us at any time. As our identity shifts through faith encounters, we will expect, possess and accomplish more. As we agree with God, the new honor opens the doors to new assignments. If our faith agrees with God's ability, but our identity still speaks against that honor—we must shatter that negative self-image. If we do not, we will still be blessed and have a long life, but it will lessen the effectiveness of our destiny.

When Saul presented Merab to David as his wife, David did not actively receive her. He should have said: "Thank you King Saul for honoring me with the hand of your daughter in marriage for my victory over Goliath. I will receive Merab as my wife at the appointed time. What a blessing from God!"

Rather he talked about himself and his family in a negative light. King Saul simply agreed with David. If we have a lesser opinion of ourselves than others do, they will eventually agree with us. Stop focusing on your family and yourself, David, and remember what God spoke over you. If David agreed with God concerning his identity, he could have walked through the open door the king of his nation was giving him.

David received Michal, the younger daughter who was lesser in the eyes of the king, rather than Merab who was promised. It originated from David's unworthiness, supported by King Saul's manipulation. Manipulation can only occur when our identity is not fully established in our Father's eyes. Our negative response to a person or an event only reveals what is left to be accomplished in us. It won't go away until we change.

When Samuel spoke over David's life he never mentioned anything about David or his family in the unworthy light. But David generated a negative image of himself and his family before King Saul. As David was playing the harp in Saul's palace, the presence of power was quite impressive. It made him feel less than what God had said about him. David received the word from Samuel about his destiny, but his identity had not yet shifted in him. Erasing the negative does not fill in the positive.

David's conversation with King Saul before facing Goliath contained nothing about his family or himself in this negative light. David's identity as a shepherd that had killed a lion and a bear allowed him to bridge by faith to being the warrior to face Goliath. He had not yet attained his identity as a king, nor could he see himself as the son-in-law of the king, though he was pursing his call to be the next king of Israel. God was working with David to synchronize his identity with his destiny, but David was not there yet. David knew he was to be the next King of Israel, yet he could not receive the king's daughter with the same confidence with which he faced the giant. It takes identity to marry the king's daughter.

Identity is a more difficult step than faith. Faith focuses on God's ability. Our identity is empowered by a sense of worthiness. That sense of worthiness is found in the presence of our Father God. *Faith believes what God can do. Identity believes what God can do through us. This is the greatest challenge we must face to reach our destiny.*

David was processing and receiving his identity to fulfill his call. That unworthy attitude left David as he fled for his life from King Saul. If we cannot receive our destiny based on our identity, others will not give it to us. David still saw himself as inferior to King Saul. Whenever Israel would worship other gods, God would allow them to suffer under those nations that worshiped those gods. His purpose was to turn Israel back to Him. We will also suffer from those things that we exalt or fear above God, until we align our identity in Him.

A man can receive nothing unless it has been given him from heaven. (John 3:27 NASB)

Earth will respond to heaven in a man. We must not agree with earth. Jesse, David's father, gave less honor to David than his other brothers. While David had faith in God, he was struggling to believe that he could be important to other people since he was not important to his father. We must agree with heaven concerning our identity, before we can receive heaven's best. We must see ourselves as sinners before we can be saved. We must see ourselves as sons before we can carry His glory.

Worthy is the Lamb who was slain to receive power and riches and wisdom and strength and honor and glory and blessing!" (Revelation 5:12 NKJV)

Jesus was worthy to receive all that is listed above. He made us worthy by His blood so we could receive heaven's best. Speak the scripture above: Jesus has made me worthy to receive power and riches and wisdom and strength and honor and glory and blessing! Until you feel worthy, you will not receive the Father's best blessings. When you receive heavens best concerning your life, you will bring glory to God as well as people. Tom Brady, quarterback of the New England Patriots and among the best quarterbacks of all time, lost all of his experienced receivers during one season. (2012-2013) He was throwing the football well, but the receivers were not experienced. Tom Brady and God had the same problem; not enough experienced receivers! Both of them can get it to us, but can we position ourselves to receive? God designs our experiences to increase our ability to receive greater gains for heaven. Isn't it great to be on His team!

Tested by Fire

Many people want David's anointing, but do not want to endure his training and testing. David made right choices in difficult situations which developed the maturity to be the king of Israel. Olympians chose to train in the hardest circumstances to attain the greatest possible strength specifically required for victory in that particular event. David's identity continued to be established in the midst of difficult situations and broken relationships as he determined to honor the Father with his life.

The words of the Lord are pure—we are not. When pure words from God enter our lives it initiates a process in the *furnace of the earth*—circumstances and relationships—to bring those words to fruition. We must go through seven major fires to allow those words to live within us and through us. It purifies identity for His purposes. Pure words call us into a more intimate walk with Him. He is burning off every thought that does not agree with His pure words so we can attain the full convergence of our destiny. The silver stays, the dross goes.

"The words of the Lord are pure words, like silver tried in a furnace of earth, purified seven times" (Ps. 12:6, NKJV).

The word must be tested in us before it operates through us. Count the major fires that you have endured. Some of us should start rejoicing, knowing the many fires we have endured are now revealing that we are very close to our destination. It becomes easier to operate in truth after the fire removes the temporal. If we allow our carnal attitudes to blow forcefully on the fires that were sent to purify our lives, they will turn into raging fires that destroy what is around us instead of dealing with what was in us. Destroying flames always blame others. Purifying flames release a fragrant worship to our Father.

We will always be fruitful on our journey to greatness, but when all of our experiences come into convergence, our fruit increases exponentially. The greater the anointing, the greater the testing will be. Qualifying as a nurse is difficult, but becoming a heart surgeon requires many more years of intensive training. God is never skimpy on training. He is committed to preparing us for His high calling on our life.

If the training is taking longer than we expected, there must be more to our purpose than God has chosen to reveal at this time. David never envisioned bringing the ark back to Jerusalem or laying out the plans for the temple that Solomon would build. He did not know that Jesus is going to sit on the throne of David. Nor did he realize that God was going to restore the Tabernacle of David in the church age that was to come. David lived beyond the covenant understanding of his day. The church is working to restore what David built and enjoyed. The idea of the temple entered his mind after he was king. We may see our call clearly, but none of us can see everything that will be revealed to us when we step into the fullness of our destiny.

When David perceived he was king, he shifted Israel forward spiritually out of the relationship he had built with God before he became king. He desired to bring the Ark of the Covenant back to Jerusalem. It takes a worshiper who is a "king" to bring the glory back into a nation. Anointing without identity cannot shift the nation.

David continued to press into the depths of God after he became king. New shifts in identity create new privileges and new activities. An engaged couple is not entitled to the same privileges as a married couple. As the same people enter a different season, different identities are received by each person. The fiancée becomes a bride. That unique new relationship encompasses new activities and goals that were dreams of faith in the past. Carry the dream until the dream carries you.

"But we have this treasure in earthen vessels, so that the surpassing greatness of the power will be of God and not from ourselves" (2 Cor. 4:7, NASB).

David treasured the words that Samuel spoke over him as a young lad. The God dreams we carry are centered in the greatness of our Father, not ours. His strategy is to release His greatness in His children to represent Him to the earth. For God so loved the world that He sent His Son. God's strategy remains the same. His heart still loves the world and He is sending His sons and daughters with His greatness to reveal Himself to the world. Jesus said if you have seen Me you have seen the Father. When the world sees us they should see the Father; particularly the part of Him we are called to represent.

The power of the Spirit of God rested on David. It takes the Holy Spirit to enter into the holy identity and holy assignments that God has revealed and promised to us. The natural man cannot receive the things of the spirit. Only the Spirit of God knows the thoughts of God. We have *not* received the spirit of this world, but the Spirit of God. The Spirit of God reveals the thoughts of God to us (1 Cor. 2:9-15). Many believers never realize that their best ideas never originated with themselves, but actually came from Spirit of God. Some God ideas contain the entire answer. Other God ideas start with seed-thought that we must develop into plans. God has chosen to work with us and through us.

"He sent a man before them, Joseph, who was sold as a slave. They afflicted his feet with fetters, He him-self was laid in irons; until the time that his word

*came to pass, the word of the Lord tested him" (Ps.
105:17–19, NASB).*

A word that is not fulfilled and seems impossible, given our
circumstances, will forge something special into our relationship with God. It will test us in a way the enemy or a problem
never could. This is a test between us and the Lord. Because
Abraham believed God as he tried to count the stars, he was
counted as a friend of God *by God*. Friends believe each other.
When we believe Father God, it deepens our friendship with
Him. God gave Joseph a dream and his brothers sold him into
his future. Potiphar's wife connected Joseph to the palace and
Pharaoh by lying to her husband. The chains of Egypt held
him, until he could wear the ring of Egypt.

Joseph never let those traumatic events change his identity. His father put so much favor on him that his brothers
and Egypt could not take it off. He was not sent to Egypt to
rule, but rather to feed his brothers who were jealous of him
and strengthen Israel. Yet Israel suffered over 400 years of
slavery in Egypt because they sold Joseph into slavery to
Egypt. When Israel carried the bones of Joseph out of Egypt
during their deliverance, Joseph's honor was fully restored
and God protected Israel.

*"For You have tried us, O God; You have refined us
as silver is refined. You brought us into the net; You
laid an oppressive burden upon our loins. You made*

men ride over our heads; we went through fire and through water, yet You brought us out into a place of abundance" (Ps. 66:10–12, NASB).

As you look at the men hiding in the cave with you, David, do you still believe what God said? Can you carry the dream to be the next king of Israel, while being hunted by the king of Israel? We see David's journey ends in abundance, but that the route is interrupted with snares, burdens, broken relationships, accusations, fires and floods. Great loss occurs on the path to abundance. Even in the natural, 80% of all present millionaires went bankrupt an average of three times. Failure is not the end—giving up is. Don't quit! Believe! Try again!

David had to endure public dishonor by Israel's king before being honored as the king himself. He was deceived, embarrassed, stolen from, and lied to by the king of Israel. A wedding is a very personal and public celebration. Being stood up by the king and the king's daughter is unthinkable. It was a deep wound that became the seedbed of bitter judgment in David's heart. The fault or sin we judge self-righteously, we will commit. What King Saul did to David, David did to Uriah. As king, David took Uriah's wife. David was a faithful servant to King Saul, just as Uriah was to King David, when the hurtful event was done by each king.

"Now Saul's daughter Michal was in love with David, and when they told Saul about it, he was pleased. 'I

will give her to him,' he thought, 'so that she may be
a snare to him and so that the hand of the Philistines
may be against him.' So Saul said to David, 'Now
you have a second opportunity to become my son-
in-law'"(1 Sam. 18:20–21, NIV).

King Saul gave David a younger daughter—a wild child—
to ruin his relationship with God. Michal was in love with
David, but she didn't love what David loved; she didn't love
worship. Was David naïve to trust King Saul who had sabo-
taged his first wedding or just rebounding from the tremendous hurt of Merab? David never inquired of God concerning
this relationship. What seemed like a natural entrance into his
destiny almost destroyed him. God never blessed this relationship, nor did He speak about it. It was manipulated by an
insecure, demonized king for ungodly, self-serving purposes.
Because David kept his eyes on God, it did not ensnare him.
What the enemy places around us is not as critical as what is
living inside us. Changing our circumstances is the least of
our problems, but they will never remain the same.

"When Saul realized that the Lord was with David and
that his daughter Michal loved David, Saul became
still more afraid of him, and he remained his enemy
the rest of his days" (1 Sam. 18:28–29, NIV).

Saul could not defeat what he feared; and neither can we. Even if we "win" in fear, the issue will simply reappear in another format. Fear will produce enemies in our lives that we cannot overcome until the fear is removed. As the Lord anoints us in a greater way, realize that there will always be those who have lost His presence and their way. Hoping to secure their own destiny, they will try to discourage, destroy or take our ministry. David never treated King Saul as an enemy or even called him his enemy, even though King Saul remained his enemy.

We must believe that God holds our destiny, not the results of conflict or competition. If we focus on fighting the people the enemy uses or protecting ourselves, God cannot get involved. He will not allow us to win with these actions and attitudes, lest it becomes a way of life. God will defend us, if we will resign from being our own lawyer and the judge. It is more about trusting Him, than winning the battle... but we must win. At what point will we stop trusting Him? Jesus trusted the Father through the cross and death. If we respond in anger to a fear-based attack, we lose ground. Peace is the response based from the security of identity that crushes the head of the serpent with bold purpose.

> *"But an evil spirit from the Lord came on Saul as he was sitting in his house with his spear in his hand. While David was playing the lyre, Saul tried to pin him to the wall with his spear, but David eluded him*

as Saul drove the spear into the wall. That night
David made good his escape" (1 Sam. 19:9,10 NIV).

To be a legendary leader we must learn how to dodge
spears. They are sharp comments designed to pin us to the
wall and destroy us. There is a time when it is proper to flee
from our present job and look for new employment! If we
overreact to the attack, we lose. If we allow those words
to pierce us, it could affect our mind or even kill our God
dreams. We do not have the authority or God's permission
to change the situation by fighting King Saul. We know that
David could have killed King Saul. David had already handled Goliath. Enduring hardships and misunderstandings
with a quieted spirit is a godly virtue. David distanced himself from Saul, but he didn't bring accusations or judgments
against Saul's rule. God used those attacks to move David
away from Saul. David's worship life allowed him to escape
personal attacks and keep them in perspective. If we can't
dodge a few spears, we may not be king material.

The jealous insecurity in Saul was trying to kill David.
David wanted to build a better relationship with Saul since he
knew he was to be the next king and he was his father-in-law,
but God was separating them to make David dependent on
Him. God didn't want David to receive His kingship from
Saul, but from heaven. God will not honor the paths of our
understanding to accomplish heaven's purpose. Instead, He
directs our path according the Spirit as we worship Him with

our very lives. Trust is worship. Your destiny is a mystery path traveled in faith; it is filled with mayhem and miracles!

Saul is told through a medium that he will die in battle the next day. David could not be in that battle with Jonathan, who would be fighting near his father's side. God had to separate David from Saul and Jonathan. Even though Jonathan loved David and knew he was to be the next king, he couldn't separate himself from the old order. Sometimes God will not let close friends accompany us into our destiny so that we learn to lean on Him totally. Close relationships of the past have the potential of invading our intimacy with God through partial dependency. It is also sometimes difficult for close friends to make the necessary shifts when there are significant role changes that can block or hinder our new sphere of authority.

"So Jonathan made a covenant with the house of David, saying, 'May the Lord call David's enemies to account.' And Jonathan had David reaffirm his oath out of love for him, because he loved him as he loved himself" (1 Sam. 20:16–17, NIV).

Jonathan was loyal to David, yet he didn't separate himself from his father, even though Saul was about to turn to witchcraft. I'm not sure it was God's plan for Jonathan to die with his father, but continual alignment with those who have departed from God's presence can give the enemy access to your life. Jonathan knew that David would be the next king of

Israel, but he did not make the transition. God used Jonathan's words to call David's enemies to account, not knowing that the enemy was actually his father, King Saul. He was soon to find out what was hidden from his eyes.

> *"Saul's anger flared up at Jonathan and he said to him, 'You son of a perverse and rebellious woman! Don't I know that you have sided with the son of Jesse to your own shame and to the shame of the mother who bore you? As long as the son of Jesse lives on this earth, neither you nor your kingdom will be estab-lished. Now send and bring him to me, for he must die!' 'Why should he be put to death? What has he done?' Jonathan asked his father. But Saul hurled his spear at him to kill him.* **Then Jonathan knew that his father intended to kill David"** *(1 Sam. 20:30–33, NIV).*

Saul insulted Jonathan's mother, his wife, and then accused Jonathan of siding with David against him. Saul told Jonathan it was shameful not to take his place as king of Israel. King Saul was operating out of a spirit of fear and anger that turned into an attempt to murder of his own son. Saul also described it as Jonathan's kingdom, because Israel had become *his kingdom.* Jonathan couldn't believe his father wanted to kill David until his father tried to kill him. Jonathan fought by his father's side in many battles. They won every battle together with the greatness that God had given them as warriors. Naturally there was a trust and a great respect built, as warriors count on each other with their very lives. It was also his father. It created a blind spot in Jonathan.

We do not know a person fully until they disagree with us. How a person handles disagreements tell us where they are in the process of inner-healing—or maturity. One of my older church leaders sat in on the last of many meetings of a disgruntled leader. After a very colorful meeting was over, the older leader told me they would not have believed that individual would have talked to me with such anger and dis- respect unless they saw it with their very own eyes. I had seen it in several meetings. As soon as they would leave me, the anger would hide in the victim mode around other members that represented sisters and brothers. Both modes were real. I was the authority that brought out the parental issues that were unresolved. The older leader was the comforting sister, who always saw the victim role, until that meeting. A leader must understand that they are called to finish what was not completed in a person's life with their father and mother; that's why leaders need a parental anointing.

In 1 Samuel 23, God asked David to defend the city of Keilah in Judah from the Philistines. David obeyed God when nothing was stable in his life. He was being hunted down by the kingdom he was destined to rule, yet God wanted David to defend that part of the same kingdom from the enemy. Can we fight for people who will refuse to protect us? David was opening their hearts for the day when he would be king of

Israel. It is interesting to note that the tribe of Judah was first to receive David as king. The victory over the Philistines at Keilah also provided David's men with much-needed provisions from the Philistines that he had defeated. David knew how to walk through conflict and confusion by keeping his eyes on God's promises and obeying His instructions even during tumultuous circumstances. David didn't "check out." He kept "his head in the game" when it was emotionally overwhelming.

Leaders mentor others by the way they walk through a crisis. More is caught than taught. It becomes a practical blueprint of truth and love that others can follow. Character and hearts are revealed and displayed during these times. Perfection is not required, but honesty is. This honesty does not mean that every person needs to have the same level of information. It is better not to inform a person with details who is not part of the problem or solution. Trust does not tell all to everyone. We can't lie to avoid a nosey spirit. Inform them that we will share the appropriate information with them if it is determined that they are part of the problem or the solution. They will recognize our integrity: truth and honor are a commitment, not a convenience and core to an influential life. God will empower us to make the correct decisions to complete the tasks assigned to us, as we walk in mercy and truth. The power of God moves with the mind of God, to fulfill the will of God. *The thoughts of God attract the power of God.* As our influence increases, there is a greater impartation and training that will be naturally released to those around us.

Chapter Seven

INFLUENCE, THE STRATEGY OF HEAVEN AND HELL

nfluence is a force that will determine the future of the Earth. God has exerted His influence from Heaven through Jesus Christ and each of His servants. Satan has released his influence from hell through his demons and servants. Many help the enemy unknowingly because of the hurts and judgments they refuse to allow God to change.

David's mighty men were directly impacted by the greatness of David. They would not have grown into their level of greatness if it had not been for his influence in their lives. As David passed each test, he raised the level of anointing on his leadership team. Likewise, Jesus' disciples would have died in obscurity had they not walked with Jesus. Who we walk with determines our future. How we walk with our spiritual father determines our authority. Even David learned how to engage in war and be a king under Saul. David could learn from King Saul, but he could not walk in his ways.

God usually doesn't call the great and the powerful to be His servants, but rather those who have a heart for Him and an eagerness to obey His will. He will build *the greatness* and *the authority* into the willing. *Israel did not birth Abraham, Abraham birthed Israel.* God created Abraham while he was still Abram. Abraham shifted the earth beyond Israel. He entered a covenant with God that reached to the church age as we are now called the "seed of Abraham." Remember, God called Abraham a father of many nations.

David's little band of rejects represented the future of the nation, and God's blessing was with them. History reveals that it is a devoted remnant that holds the keys to the future of the earth. All major shifts in the earth started with a few people that ended in a landslide of influence. On the 31st of October 1517, Martin Luther posted the ninety-five theses on the door of the Castle Church of Wittenberg, according to university custom. Luther did not know that it would radically change the church forever. David worshipped the Lord as a young shepherd, not realizing he was called to restore worship back to Israel.

After Saul returned from pursuing the Philistines, he was told, "David is in the Desert of En Gedi." So Saul took three thousand able young men from all Israel and set out to look for David and his men near *the Crags of the Wild Goats. He came to the sheep pens along the way; a cave was there, and Saul went in to relieve himself. David and his men were far back in the cave. The men said, "This is the day the Lord spoke of when he said to you, **'I will give your enemy into your hands for you to deal with as you wish.'"** Then David crept up unnoticed and cut off a corner of Saul's robe. Afterward, David was conscience-stricken for having cut off a corner of his robe. He said to his men, "The Lord forbid that I should do such a thing to my master, the Lord's anointed, or lay my hand on him; for he is the anointed of the Lord." **With these words David sharply rebuked his men and did not allow them to attack Saul.** And Saul left the cave and went his way. (1 Sam. 24:1–7, NIV).*

When David cut Saul's robe, it stirred up murder in the hearts of the men who followed him. When he saw them rise to attack King Saul, David recognized that he had started it by cutting off a corner of Saul's robe. His open repentance for what he had done preceded his rebuke to his men. A leader's repentance sets the tone for the followers. A leader's actions, great or small, good or evil, are amplified in the behavior of their followers. It is recorded in Numbers 12 that Miriam and Aaron opposed Moses and several chapters later Israel rebelled against Moses. They followed the attitude of the leaders next to Moses.

David cut off the corner of the king's mantle—a mantle that he was soon to wear. When we start destroying the mantle that God has promised us, it shows a lack of honor for it and those wearing it. God has set them in authority. It also displays a lack of respect for heaven's timing. If God had chosen to remove Saul's mantle at that time, he didn't need David's help.

The way we treat our predecessor in front of our followers determines how they will later treat us. David understood the principle of honor, as well as the principle of sowing and reaping. David's men protected him as he protected Saul. We must honor the mantle we are called to inherit even if the person wearing it is King Saul. If we keep cutting their mantle, what will be left of it when we receive it? If we respect the mantle and the position, even if the person is not worthy of respect in our eyes, it will bring honor to our name in our season. Putting others down never advances our greatness. If we align with the accuser of the brethren, we lose the anointing and the heart of Father God.

It is interesting to note that God told David that He would put his enemy in his hand to do with as he wished. God did not say what David should do, but rather indicated that He would see the desire in David's heart. The Father was going deeper into David's life than sheer obedience. He was testing the desire of David's heart. Would he be like Jesus, sparing and saving those who desired to kill Him? Twice David showed forth the mercy of God, over judgment. Scripture speaks in

Isaiah 9 that Jesus will sit on the "throne of David." One of the reasons this will occur is because David spared the lives of those who tried to kill him, just like Jesus.

Fading Hope, Increased Frustration

"Then Samuel died; and the Israelites gathered together and lamented for him, and buried him at his home in Ramah. And David arose and went down to the Wilderness of Paran" (1 Sam. 25:1 NKJV).

David's spiritual link to the throne was dead! Why didn't God keep Samuel alive to give witness to all of Israel that God had chosen David in his youth to be the next king of Israel? The one person who could have been the greatest help to David was now dead. God didn't allow Jonathan to be there either. Jonathan would have been another convincing voice for David to be accepted as king, since he was the heir apparent to the throne. God will not allow our call to rest on the help of men, though others must bear witness. David's hope was fading, and frustration was beginning to set in his heart.

In 1 Samuel 25, David sent some his men to ask Nabal for provisions. David's men had guarded Nabal's flocks from harm, but Nabal insulted David and his men, giving them nothing. Then he accused David of rebellion and unfaithfulness—just as King Saul was. Saul stripped David of all his rewards and now Nabal was doing the same thing. Offenses that are linked with unhealed past hurts are the most volatile and impossible to control. David lost it.

> *David had just said, **"It's been useless**—all my watching over this fellow's property in the wilderness so that nothing of his was missing. He has paid me back evil for good. May God deal with David, be it ever so severely, if by morning I leave alive one male of all who belong to him!" (1 Sam. 25:21,22 NIV)*

Did you ever feel like everything you have done has been useless? David did! What difference did it make that he killed Goliath? He was no longer a hero in Israel, but the hunted villain. What did it accomplish to lead the armies of Israel into victorious battles? All David's honor seemed stripped away. "I served King Saul and now he is trying to kill me. My wife, Michal, has been given to another man. I have spared and honored the life of King Saul, but nothing is working! And now this insolent man will not even give me and my men a few sheep after all we have done for him. To top it off, he is accusing me of being a rebel!" David's frustration turned to anger and then to murder. God spoke through Abigal so David could reconsider his decision to avenge himself!

> *"And now, my lord, as surely as the Lord your God lives and as you live, **since the Lord has kept you from bloodshed and from avenging yourself with your***

own hands, *may your enemies and all who are intent on harming my lord be like Nabal. And let this gift, which your servant has brought to my lord, be given to the men who follow you. Please forgive your servant's presumption.* **The Lord your God will certainly make a lasting dynasty for my lord, because you fight the Lord's battles, and no wrongdoing will be found in you as long as you live.** *Even though someone is pursuing you to take your life, the life of my lord will be bound securely in the bundle of the living by the Lord your God, but the lives of your enemies he will hurl away as from the pocket of a sling.* **When the Lord has fulfilled for my lord every good thing he promised concerning him and has appointed him ruler over Israel,** *my lord will not have on his conscience the staggering burden of needless bloodshed or of having avenged himself.* **And when the Lord your God has brought my lord success, remember your servant."** *David said to Abigail, "Praise be to the Lord, the God of Israel, who has sent you today to meet me.* **May you be blessed for your good judgment and for keeping me from bloodshed this day and from avenging myself with my own hands.** *Otherwise, as surely as the Lord, the God of Israel, lives, who has kept me from harming you, if you had not come quickly to meet me, not one male belonging to Nabal would have been left alive by daybreak." (1 Sam. 25:26–34)*

We see David's frustration with his situation. He was not being recognized or rewarded for any of his efforts. He was about to "fix the problem" by the strength of his own hand instead of waiting on God's hand. David's oath is similar to Jezebel's in 1 Kings 19:1–2 when she vows to kill Elijah. Clearly, David wasn't operating out of a godly spirit, but a controlling spirit that operates in all men when they fail to trust God and rely on themselves. God had already determined to kill Nabal, but David was about to beat Him to the punch. When David stopped his plan with Nabal, then God took care of it. There are certain issues that we must wait for God to resolve, even when we have the power and ability to do it ourselves. The results were much better when David left it in God's hands. David received Abigail as his wife and all of Nabal's wealth. The men he would have killed needlessly then served him.

Our integrity is often displayed by what we refuse to do. Sometimes it feels like we're way long overdue to obtain the next step in our destiny. Everything can seem to be drifting away instead of coming closer. During such periods, we can become afraid, frustrated or frantic. We cannot cave into those emotions or give place to avenge or advance ourselves. We must stand firm and remind God that we believe what He said as conditions deteriorate. David, you are the future king of Israel, not the godfather of the Mafia!

We remember our identity in hard times and act accordingly. Chosen actions reveal our identity. Our identity should also be the determiner of our actions. We should always make decisions based on the Christ in us, the hope of glory. We make our decisions with His Word and Spirit and follow through with all that He has invested in us. It will open the doors to our destiny in the heavens. In the right time, God will open the doors on the earth. We must navigate the gates in heaven to access the doors on earth.

Nabal's wife, Abigail, went out to meet David and bowed down before him as he and his men were coming to kill Nabal and all his men. She asked for forgiveness for Nabal as she brought more food than David had originally requested. She also reminded David to fight the Lord's battles, and not his own. It was known throughout Israel that David had resisted killing King Saul when he had the opportunity. People were talking about the great heart of David, the next king of Israel. God gave him an update through Abigail.

Notice the progression of truths in Abigail's speech: The Lord has kept you from bloodshed. You fight the Lord's battles. When the Lord fulfills every good promise for my lord and appoints you as ruler over Israel, you will not carry in your conscience the guilt of needless bloodshed. Remember me when the Lord has brought you success.

Abigail released honor to David by calling him lord. Honor is very healing to the discouraged and broken. For the first time David was hearing a common ordinary person in Israel confirming that he would be king. Hope was arising in David at a point of great frustration. God was doing a work in Israel that was hidden from David's eyes until this moment. God will give us the encouragement we need along the way, but let Him be the source for our journey. If encouragement is the only thing that keeps us in the journey, it becomes an idol. David needed it, but he didn't live for it.

Abigail inspired David to do the right thing. Everyone needs an Abigail in their moments of frustration. God is our defender and vindicator. Taking matters into our own hands shows a lack of trust and actually is a judgment against God. It goes something like this: "God, You are doing a poor job managing my life and career promises at this present time. I couldn't have made it here without You. Thanks for Your help, but I have it covered from here to the throne of Israel. I can handle this."

The closer we get to our destiny, the greater the resistance and frequency of tests. The closer it comes, the harder it is to resist making it happen. When it seems as if all hell breaks loose, we keep pressing forward. We are about to go through a very important door to our destiny.

So David and Abishai went to the army by night, and there was Saul, lying asleep inside the camp with his spear stuck in the ground near his head. Abner and the soldiers were lying around him. Abishai said to David, "Today God has delivered your enemy into your hands. Now let me pin him to the ground with one thrust of my spear; I won't strike him twice." But

David said to Abishai, "Don't destroy him! Who can
lay a hand on the Lord's anointed and be guiltless? As
surely as the Lord lives," he said, "the Lord himself
will strike him; either his time will come and he will
die, or he will go into battle and perish. But the Lord
forbid that I should lay a hand on the Lord's anointed.
(1 Sam. 26:7-11, NIV)

Here, David was tested at a higher level. What would he
do when the Lord created the opportunity to promote himself? The Lord had put Saul and all his men into a deep sleep.
It seemed like this scenario proved that it was God's will for
David to allow Abishai to kill King Saul to advance him into
his promised destiny. Only one man was with him. There
were no other witnesses, but David knew he would be guilty
if he allowed Abishai to kill Saul. When David refused to
allow Abishai to kill King Saul, he spoke of himself laying
a hand on the Lord's anointed. David did not refer to Saul's
name, but rather who had anointed Saul to keep his perspective. David took responsibility for his men's decisions he per-
mitted as if it were his actions. That is a mark of a great leader.

Abigail's words strengthened David before this difficult test. God was watching closely. David was a man after
God's own heart and would do whatever God asked him to do.
David also refused to do what God did not speak at a time of
unusual opportunity for personal benefit, while under intense
pressure from King Saul and encouragement from his friend.

How we come into power is how we will stay in power. If we kill to get it, we'll have to kill to keep it. Likewise, if we trust God to get it, we must continue to trust Him to keep it. We can't let our carnal desire to fulfill our destiny make a killer out of us. We need to be like David, *a lover of God and a protector of Saul*. Have you ever protected someone that is trying to kill you? That determines if we are truly a David. It's easier for us to kill Goliath than to protect our Saul. In the heat of the battles of life, our identity will be forged by our choices.

Living with the Enemy

David went from leading the armies of Israel to being hunted down by those very same men. Everyone must go through a time of being dishonored and criticized by those whom they had developed favor and position that seemed like the sure path to their destiny. It is a "David" test. Can we still believe for our destiny when our obvious ladder to success has been burnt? Will we give into bitterness and hatred?

David married one of the King's daughters and it seemed to be a very natural step to make Samuel's prophecy closer and more secure. David was already great friends with Jonathan, the king's son. Marrying the king's daughter shifted David's identity in the eyes of Israel as he became a part of the royal family, but it was not the easy step to become the next king of Israel. David required that Michal, the king's daughter, to be returned to him as his wife to secure his throne when he became king of Israel. David had to overcome the trauma of his wife being given to another man by his Father-in-law.

At one point in my ministry, I received incredible promotion and honor from a group of people, and years later it fell apart. Having expected to be ushered into my destiny through that situation, I questioned God. He replied, "You were looking for them to promote you to the next level. The only reason you were offended by their actions is because you looked to them as your source. I could not allow it to work for you. It would have limited your future and our relationship. They could never do for you what I have planned for your future."

My view of the entire event totally shifted. Rather than focusing on my offenses, hurts, and questions, I began to comprehend more of God's unending love and the greatness of His plans for my life. I had shifted my faith in God for my destiny, to focusing on what they would do for me.

Years later, God restored that relationship and it has become greater than I ever could have imagined. I realize now that God was more interested in the issues He had with me than the issues I had with them. That was an amazing revelation. Our pain is connected to our issues, not theirs. Jesus wasn't hurt by what people said to Him as He was dying on the cross. He was connected to God's heart, not the false accusations against Him. He was living in loving obedience to the Father, refusing to dwell in the rejection and hatred that surrounded Him. When we chose who we will serve, it limits who can hurt us. Pain is self-centered by nature. If you throw a pity party, demons who bring more torment will attend.

David started building his "mighty men" in the cave of Adullam (1 Sam. 22). He was a restorer of hope in the midst of a personally dark time. All of us must raise others up when we are at a point of personal weakness and unsure about our future. We must be willing to pray for others in areas where we have not yet received a breakthrough. We must keep training up others and helping them, even when our own future seems questionable in our own eyes. It is required of those who desire to be like David.

> *Then Saul said to David, "May you be blessed, David my son;* **you will do great things and surely triumph."** *So David went on his way, and Saul returned home.* **But David thought to himself, "One of these days I will be destroyed by the hand of Saul.** *The best thing I can do is to escape to the land of the Philistines. Then Saul will give up searching for me anywhere in Israel, and I will slip out of his hand." (1 Samuel 26:25-1 Samuel 27:1)*

The pain in David's life was beginning to affect his thoughts and faith. King Saul actually had more faith concerning David's life at this point in time than David! "The best thing I can do" is not always the God thing. David could not see the end to the problems; he could only see the end of his life. There comes a point in life where the battles become so intense and so unending that we view them as our life. It is interesting how many revivals were ushered in by pastors who were ready to quit. When we come to the end of ourselves, we step into the beginnings of God. Then all that happens rests on Him and not on us or our plans.

It is dangerous when we start thinking to ourselves without the presence and promises of God. First of all, we have pushed God out of the process and the equation. There is a lot of grey matter between our ears, and it is very easy to get stuck in one of our grey thoughts. Our mind was designed to contain the mind of Christ. Without the thoughts of Christ, our mind is a dangerous place to visit. It will work against the plans of God, not with them.

We must press into God's presence and have our mind filled with His thoughts. We have the mind of Christ through the Spirit of God, the heart of God, and His Word. The mind of Christ is fully integrated when our thoughts, responses, and actions reflect Him. The thoughts of Christ lead to the ways of Christ.

David went from defeating the enemies of Israel to hiding among them and pretending to be their friend. David had been fleeing King Saul, hiding throughout Israel. The hunt was so severe that David resorted to hiding with the enemy in the land of the enemy. David actually lived one step between life and death on several occasions. King Saul would have to engage war with the Philistines just to search for David in the land of the enemy. Several years earlier, David actually resorted to acting insane before Achish the first time in order to save his life from him. The Philistines believed that if you kill an insane person, it would bring bad luck. So Achish sent David away (1 Sam. 21:10-15). This time David presented himself to Achish as the enemy of King Saul and Israel. Since it was known that King Saul was hunting for David throughout the nation to kill him, Achish would understandably believe that David was against King Saul and Israel.

Achish's name means "anger." David lived next to "anger" without allowing it to change his spirit. At this point in David's life the enemy was treating him better than God's people. David lived with Achish for one year and four months and did not allow the hatred that Achish had for God, King Saul and Israel to touch his heart. It was difficult for David to keep the hurts of King Saul from turning into anger, when he lived with a person who literally wanted to destroy Saul.

David had to keep his heart true to the vision that God had promised him. Bitterness was knocking at David's door, but he kept his heart pure. When you excuse your bad attitude because of what others have done, you need to see the importance of the love of God when there are no natural reasons present except God, Himself. Be a David! David dwelt in God, accessing the love of God, resisting the spirits that harassed Saul and the anger of Achish. That is a narrow path to navigate.

There are times when nothing makes sense. In those times, we must still remember who we are in God and who He is to us. There is no logical place to file certain traumatic experiences. If we try to mentally process these traumatic events without God's love and power it will push us towards the edge of insanity. *Jesus is the answer* when we see no answer. Those traumatic events will steal our rest if we do not lay them at the feet of Jesus. Unhealthy emotions emerge if we do not forgive and release. We must choose not to accept any of the dark baggage that comes with those traumatic events. There is no logic to the abuse or pains that result from a fallen world of sin and the evil nature of Satan. Explanations do not bring healing; just better understanding. The only place of rest is in God alone. In Psalms, we're exhorted to "Be still, and know that I am God."

David had killed Goliath, the champion of the Philistine army, twelve years prior to hiding with the Philistines. To have David on their side was a trophy to their greatness. It also gave them relief, knowing they wouldn't have to face him in battle. David led Achish to believe that he was attacking the villages of Israel. In actuality, David was destroying other towns nearby. Despite his struggle with hopelessness, David kept on doing the right things. Another dimension of faith is displayed by your actions in the midst of hopelessness.

Saul lost his personal relationship with God while living in the destiny that God had ordained for him. David kept his relationship with God when he was being denied his position and honor. Never let your destiny become your god.

Devastation before Destination

David and his men reached Ziklag on the third day. Now the Amalekites... had attacked Ziklag and burned it, [2] and had taken captive the women and everyone else in it, both young and old. They killed none of them, but carried them off as they went on their way.[3] When David and his men reached Ziklag, they found it destroyed by fire and their wives and sons and daughters taken captive. [4] So David and his men wept aloud until they had no strength left to weep. [5] David's two wives had been captured... [6] David was greatly distressed because the men were talking of stoning him; each one was bitter in spirit because of his sons and daughters. But David found strength in the LORD his God. [8] ...and David inquired of the LORD, "Shall I pursue this raiding party? Will I overtake them?" "Pursue them," he answered. "You will certainly overtake them and succeed in the rescue."(1Sam30:1-8)

Achish required David to go with him into battle against King Saul and Israel as his personal bodyguard. Achish joined the other Philistine commanders who refused to let David fight with them. They feared that in the heat of the battle David would turn against them to gain favor back with King Saul. It had already been revealed to King Saul that he and his sons would die in this battle and Israel would be defeated. David had already refused to kill King Saul twice when he had easy opportunities.

David and his men were in a very awkward situation. Israel would be fighting in the name of God and the Philistines in the name of their gods. David's men may not have been happy with the way David handled this situation. I am sure they were asking David why they are going with Achish to fight against their own people. David could not refuse to go with Achish, yet he could not fight against Israel. David was trusting God to work it out. After traveling to the place where the Philistine kings were gathered, there was a long debate among the Philistine kings concerning David.

The Philistine kings refused to allow David to join the battle. David and his men arrived home three days later. It seemed like such a waste of time. The men were tired and hungry. When the city came into view, everything had been burnt to the ground. Their wives, children and possessions were all gone. They were overwhelmed with grief and anger. If they had not left with David, this would have never happened! They were very upset with David and his leadership. They talked of stoning him among themselves. God will take us to zero, before He takes us to hero.

David had to overcome the bitterness and betrayal of his mighty men when he was at a personal place of great loss as well. David strengthened himself in the Lord before he inquired of the Lord. The promise of victory was not the key to David strengthening himself, which had not yet been revealed. It was the presence of the Lord that David pursued. The Lord was David's portion, not his victory over the enemy.

David then inquired of the Lord. He put his men's eyes back on God and His instruction. David did not waste time defending his decisions of the past week. God spoke and David responded with faith when one third of the men were so tired that they could not even make the journey to the battle, let alone fight. David now had to keep his faith and attitude fixed as he experienced a "Gideon" reduction in the small band of warriors.

Can we win with less? Can we still believe God's promised victory as our army downsizes from exhaustion? It was not a separation of the holy from the unholy as we see the anger of those who went with David not wanting to share the reward of the victory. The scripture records that there were some evil men and trouble makers in the band of mighty warriors. David fought from morning until evening to receive the promised victory. Still four hundred young men escape on camels! David only had four hundred men. God is our strength when we have no strength. If we are outnumbered, don't worry, He has us covered.

My wife of twenty six years passed away after a two year battle with cancer. I was mentally exhausted. Two weeks before she passed away the four church members that worked the closest with her informed us they were going to be a part of a new church that was being formed by another church member who did not meet with us. Several of the leaders in the church thought that I should travel full time as a prophet and apostle and they should pick the next pastor.

When I remarried they directly opposed my wife, LuAnne, having any role in the church even though God had clearly brought her to the church for His purposes. God brought LuAnne into my life in such a supernatural way to help break the grief that was still griping me and the church. You can read about it in, "God, I Feel Like Cinderella!" It is a story of restoration and miracles that has already touched tens of thousands around the world.

There were many challenges I was personally facing in the midst of a new joy. I had to strengthen myself in the Lord. When you face things you never expected, you have the opportunity to find God in a way you never knew Him before. It was the best of times and the worst of times. In the midst of this time some of my friends gave me incredible support. Others actually positioned themselves against me. Others said nothing. God became the strength of my heart in a deeper way than I had ever experienced. It will always be a highlight in my life of my personal relationship with Father God taking me to another level of intimacy with Him.

Chapter Eight

A NEW PLACE TO DWELL

It happened after this that David inquired of the Lord,
saying, "Shall I go up to any of the cities of Judah?"
And the Lord said to him, "Go up." David said,
"Where shall I go up?" And He said, "To Hebron."
So David went up there ... and dwelt in the cities of
Hebron. Then the men of Judah came, and there they
anointed David king over the house of Judah" (2 Sam.
2:1–4, NKJV).

God allowed Ziklag to burn to the ground to make sure that David did not return to that place of hiding, given to him by the enemy. After that time however, Ziklag always belonged to Judah! David came to dwell in Ziklag because he thought that King Saul was going to destroy him. When we lose vision we dwell in places that He has not chosen for us. Our destiny has a geographical location as well as spiritual position. There are geographical locations that can actually accelerate or hinder what God has planned for us. David made that decision out of disappointment and fear.

Not long after David started thinking to himself that Saul was going to destroy him, Father God removed Saul. God's faithfulness was revealed to David at his darkest time. David had regained his implicit faith that what God said was coming to pass. God loves to take us from the prison to the palace, from Ziklag to Hebron. David knew it was time to find a new dwelling place.

When David heard that King Saul was dead, he inquired of the Lord if he should go up to Judah. The Lord told him to go up. The Father did not tell him where in Judah until David asked. The Father will tell you more details if you ask Him. Some believers only want a "yes" or a "no" and then they take over from there. The Father wants His sons to invite Him into their lives. Hebron is a very interesting place. Abraham made his home there and Joshua assigned it to Caleb. Abraham, Isaac and Jacob are buried there. Jewish tradition holds that Adam and Eve are buried there as well. God is taking David into a place of beginnings and history to extend and fulfill the dreams and faith of those who went before him.

David could not take the throne of Israel that was prophesied after he killed Goliath. He could not take it after he killed ten thousands and the king only killed a thousand. Outperforming the king was not an indicator that David was ready to rule. David could not take the throne when he had the opportunity to kill the king, nor could he allow his men to do it for him, even if the king was trying to kill David. These are the rules in the Kingdom of God. David honored them and God honored David.

It takes a particular strength to resist doing it the wrong way, but a greater strength to do it the right way. David, today is your day to step into your future. You must present yourself in Judah, a place of praise. It is now your day to rule! Because you did not take matters into your hands, now I am putting it into your hands. My hand is on you, David. I am your Father God and you are My son, a king. This is the place and time where you will be received and celebrated as you step into your destiny... by some.

Partial Fulfillment

"Now therefore, let your hands be strong and be val-iant; for Saul your lord is dead, and also the house of Judah has anointed me king over them." **But Abner the son of Ner, commander of Saul's army, had taken Ish-bosheth the son of Saul** *and brought him over to Mahanaim. He made him king... even over all Israel. Ish-bosheth, Saul's son, was forty years old when he became king over Israel, and he was king for two years. The house of Judah, however, followed David (2 Samuel 2:7-11 NASB).*

Saul was dead, but the spirit that was blocking David's destiny was not. We must understand the enemy is real. We wrestle not against flesh and blood, but spiritual powers of darkness. When we step toward our identity and purpose, resistance is normal. Abner did not want to give up his sphere of influence to allow David to come forward as king of all Israel.

A civil war arose in Israel when David was made king at Judah. We should never expect everyone to celebrate and receive what God has called us to do. As soon as David was accepted as king in Judah, Abner (King Saul's military leader) raised up King Saul's son to king over Israel to save his job and influence in the land. That was a ton of rejection for David to experience as he first stepped into fulfilling his destiny as king of Israel. Will we keep moving forward when others walk away?

Civil war carries a very high level of opposition. Everyone must learn how to live in the swirl of human opinions. Partial fulfillment can drive us to discouragement. When David was anointed by Samuel, he never saw the journey to obtain the keys of his identity, just the promise. God is big on the call, but small on the details. Trusting God will always be the backbone to the dreams of destiny. When we don't know what's going on, we still must go on.

Less than six months after I became pastor, the church doubled in members. The former pastor started treating me differently. There was a point where he mentally broke down and confessed that he was jealous of me. Three days later it was just the same as before. I asked the former pastor to release me to lead the church or I would turn the church and pastorate back over to him and leave that area. They decided I should leave. I was so happy to have this year-long battle over! I went to church to preach my resignation sermon and leave. I called him to ask how he would like to designate the offering that Sunday, since it was now his church.

He called me back ten minutes before the service and said he had changed his mind; he would keep the building, I could have the people. The relief of joy turned into tears as I knew that God was not releasing me to leave. The building we were meeting in was worth over $400,000. That was gone. The Lord spoke so clearly to go buy land. We only had $50.00 in our checking account. There was no need to have a board meeting at that point—there was nothing to talk about. Within three months we purchased 42 acres of farm land. Twenty-five years later we sold 30 acres. The value of each acre increased thirty times to the penny of the original price.

I remember weeping over the $400,000 that was lost as I tried to plan my future, but I am not weeping anymore. In our darkest times, God's greatest miracles occur. God gave the church the land to keep me here, even though we did not build until 15 years later. I'd rather have $50 and a word from God than $400,000 and my own plans. If we keep our heart right, God makes our crooked paths straight and blesses us. God was building my identity while I was building a church.

Family wars are destiny destroyers that release depression and hopelessness. They are the wars you would never pick, but ones which you must win. The house of David grew stronger and the house of Saul grew weaker. David didn't gain from their weakness, David gained from his strength. There are battles we must engage to shift our destiny from partial to complete fulfillment. These are battles that we must win gently, but win we must. Someday you will rule over those who opposed you, David. Win gently.

David had been king over Judah for seven years and six months (2 Sam. 5:5) when the elders of Israel came to Hebron to anoint David as king over Israel. We may know our destiny, but it must be confirmed by others, including the house of Saul. We don't have many accounts of the battles between the two houses, but David warred with an awareness that the opposition would later have to receive him as their king. You don't war with family like they're the enemy or they will never receive your leadership. David never referred to Saul as his enemy to others.

David wept for Saul and Jonathan upon hearing of their deaths. David honored those who buried King Saul with honor after he was killed. They removed his body that was hanging on the enemy's wall, giving King Saul a proper burial. David received great honor because he gave honor to those who did not honor him. Do not allow how people treat you to change the way God has called you to live.

David's White House

"Now Hiram king of Tyre sent messengers to David,
and timber of cedars, with masons and carpenters,
to build him a house. **And David perceived that the**
Lord had confirmed him king *over Israel, for his*
kingdom was lifted up on high, because of his people
Israel" *(1 Chron. 14:1–2, KJV).*

After David was anointed as king of Israel, he led his men in unprecedented triumph over the Jebusites. Joshua and Caleb did not drive them out or the many leaders that followed them. The Jebusites were mocking David as he came into the fullness of his destiny. The place where God has called us to rule from is the last place the enemy ever wants us to possess.

If we can take it from that mocking spirit, we will be able to break the power of the enemy off the people and the land. The last thing the enemy wants us to attain is our throne of authority. He would rather give up victories to us as long as he can possess our place of authority. The purpose and plans of God always require a man who will walk with His authority on the earth. The serpent was not after the Garden of Eden, he was after Adam's identity.

David captured Jerusalem and renamed it the City of David. Despite his victories, David continued to struggle with accepting his new identity. It seemed like everything he ever obtained was always stripped away. The traumas of his journey were now blocking his view and creating a mindset that needed to be shifted and God knew it. Our Father God will send us those we need to build a house of honor to help us to break off the dishonor from the past seasons. It will elevate our identity and release our purpose. That honor will bring a profound deep healing to our heart.

David had the crown on his head and yet he still did not perceive that the Lord had confirmed him king over Israel! Didn't he remember that Samuel had anointed him to be king over Israel when he was a boy? Had David forgotten about Goliath and the many great victories that caused others to see him as their future leader?

David was the greatest king Israel ever had. Yet he struggled to enter into agreement with his promised kingship as the crown rested on his head! If we don't shift our mindset to match our "now season," our actions won't match our purpose and position. Then our effectiveness and our productivity will be restricted by our perception. Our awareness of who we are is directly linked with our ability to dream, think, and move with God. God's dream for our life is greater than ours. We must see ourselves as He does to enter His dreams.

Could it be that many believers are standing in their place of promised destiny and yet cannot perceive it? If it happened to David, the greatest king of Israel, it has happened to all of us at one point of our life or another. How did this come about in David's life? God is not just giving us insight concerning David, but an insight into each of our lives.

David had a very difficult journey to the throne. Things were promised, but not delivered. What he received was later taken from him. It seemed as if there was nothing that David could count on in his life. David fled from Saul until he was thirty years old. Many of his life tests occurred while in his twenties. David was stuck in past experiences. Was this just another victory that would unravel in a few months?

David's kingdom was far from secure. A civil war had just ended, and there were those who still didn't want to see David reign. He was not living in the land of his tribe, Judah, as he ruled all Israel. He ruled from the city that resisted him at two different levels; His people and the enemy. If David did not fully enter into his new identity, he would be very vulnerable to those who disliked him. God will never allow everyone to like us. If we do not agree with God on who we are to Him, someone else will cause our mind to agree with them and we will not like the results. It's not their fault. It's ours. We would not agree with God.

The crown was set on his head, but it still wasn't established in his thoughts, his vision, or his actions. David had reached God's goal and his destiny, but he had not yet perceived that the Lord had established him as king over Israel. Father God sent King Hiram to help David settle this issue.

"King Hiram of Tyre sent an envoy to David...to build him a royal palace. (1 Chron. 14:1MSG).

It takes a king to build a "White House." David could never have built his own "White House." He would have built an *upgraded shepherd's shack*. God took a man who was already a king to bring revelation to David that he was now a king too! That "White House" provided an atmosphere of honor and authority to shift David's identity.

Hiram's name means "my brother is exalted" or "brother of the exalted one." Isn't that amazing? Hiram's life purpose was embedded in his name. God created Hiram to exalt David at the right time to establish destiny in David's mind. What Samuel birthed in David as he spoke God's words over him as a young boy, Hiram finished as he built David his "White House." God has created your "Hiram" to help establish you and your call at the precise time. God used a sun-worshipping Pharaoh to make Joseph's God dream come true. These will not be people you selected, they will be unforeseen people picked by God.

After years of strategizing, the best campaigner becomes the next President of the United States of America, not the best politician. After they are sworn into office, *they are required to live in the White House.* They are not allowed to live in their own house, even if it is larger and costs more. Every morning they wake up in the White House, it helps forge their new identity. It reminds them that they are the

President of the United States of America. It was built for that purpose. As their identity shifts, the purpose of that office becomes more natural.

Each salute, each mode of transportation, every room speaks to the activity and purpose of the President of the United States of America. There is the Oval Office, conference rooms, security centers and rooms to engage and entertain the leaders of other nations. The White House is a place that forges the campaigner into the president. Where we live determines our identity in so many ways. Our "White House" is specifically designed to support the purposes and activities that God has determined for us to accomplish. We can't allow the jealousy of others or an unworthy spirit within us to block us from living in our "White House." King Jesus built that house for us. Live in it! It cost Him His life to build it. Jesus, the Son of God, was forsaken so that we could be restored as "sons."

There comes a time in every David's life when God uses another king to build us a "White House." This shifts our identity into our purpose and activities. We must live in and operate from our "White House." We must refuse to live in what we have built. Live in what King Jesus has built for us. He will use other "kings" to build it for us. It will bring a greater honor, releasing a greater anointing in our life. The purpose of our destiny is to bless Him and those He puts in our life. We must do it with all of our heart!

"Now Hiram king of Tyre sent messengers to David, and timber of cedars, with masons and carpenters, to build him a house. And David perceived that the Lord had confirmed him king over Israel, for his kingdom was lifted up on high, because of his people Israel. And David took more wives at Jerusalem: and David begat more sons and daughters" (1 Chron. 14:1–3, KJV).

As David's identity was established as king, he began birthing more sons and daughter to secure his kingdom, as every king in those days would do. If he were overthrown, the number of sons and daughters would secure his kingdom from the enemy. In God's Kingdom, He is anointing kings who will raise up many spiritual sons and daughters to secure and expand His Kingdom. The spirit of Elijah is being released into the earth for the greatest revival ever seen.

Always With You

"Thus says the Lord of hosts: **"I took you from the sheepfold, from following the sheep, to be ruler over My people, over Israel. And I have been with you wherever you have gone, and have cut off all your enemies from before you, and have made you a great name, like the name of the great men who are on the earth..."** *(2 Sam. 7:8–9, NKJV).*

The Lord is speaking to David after he had been king for many years. He is reminding David where He took him from to become ruler over Israel. It seems as if God is smiling as He recounts David's beginning; "You first started as a shepherd boy that did not even have the skill to lead the sheep; you were simply following them." Nothing great ever happened as a shepherd boy until after Samuel anointed David. Father God is letting David know that all the greatness of his leadership and the glory of the kingdom of Israel came from Him.

Many great leaders never saw themselves as leaders when they were younger, but Father God made them great. After experiencing greatness, we must totally focus on our Great Father. When God takes you from the sheepfold to the throne remember that it is not based on your talent or your personal greatness. David could not take credit for his journey; he could only give praise to God. Father God made David, His son, great and famous. The Lord of hosts knew the environment, identity and activities from which He took David. God wanted David to grasp his life journey from God's viewpoint.

The Lord informed David that He has been with him on every part of his journey. This was an update from heaven, not confirming what David already knew. David didn't always know it— nor do we. God was with David through every disappointment and trauma. God was there when David could not sense Him nor see Him. The Father wanted to cover that issue with David. There is a time that God will have us reflect on our lives with an update from heaven. The answer to every situation is not the key; but knowledge of His presence with us in the dark times is life-altering.

God said that He cut all of David's enemies off before him. I know that David was so glad he didn't. So was God. It was not David's great warrior anointing that accomplished this feat. Our Father takes care of the enemy.

It was the Father's joy to make David's name great in the earth. That is our Father God! He gives His greatness to His sons and daughters.

David's Song

> *Psalm 21 (A Psalm of David For The Choir)*
> *O LORD, in Your strength the king will be glad,*
> *³ᵇ You set a crown of fine gold on his head.*
> *⁵ᵇ Splendor and majesty You place upon him.*
> *⁷ For the king trusts in the LORD,*
> *And through the lovingkindness of the Most High he will not be shaken.*

David is now speaking of himself in the third person. *The king* is rejoicing in Your strength. David was not rejoicing in his strength, but the Lord's. David took no credit for the strength that was now a part of his life as king of Israel. David was glad in the strength of the Lord, not measuring his as some do. Yet David clearly sees himself as "the king."

Judah and Israel had set the crown on David's head, but David recognized that it was Father God that had set the crown of fine gold on his head. It doesn't matter that other people were a huge factor in this event; David gave praise to God for the authority and position in life that God had entrusted to him. David knew it was God who gave him the splendor and majesty to walk as a king. He did not take credit for reaching goals that he had set or believed to obtain.

David declared that *the king* trusts in the Lord. He did not trust in the greatness God had given him among men on the earth, but he trusted in the greatness of his God. Because of Your loving kindness, *the king* will not be shaken. David now lived above the traumas of his life because of Father God's love. He now speaks of being *the king* with a tremendous revelation of the Father in each aspect, in each verse above.

Note that this song was written by King David for the choir to sing. Why would he want them to sing it? First of all, for him! He needed to have his spirit and mind saturated with this view of his life. David had secured his identity in Father God. He was also securing his identity and purpose with open worship to resist the attacks of the enemy that would certainly face his kingdom.

David worshiped God for who God was. David also worshiped God for who God had made *him*. David conquered the identity crisis that the serpent created in the Garden of Eden, against God, Adam and Eve, with his song of praise. David overcame the identity crisis from the Garden of Eden and gained his destiny. Now he possessed the "City of David." David made his identity a matter of deep worship to Father God. *Our identity is the key to our destiny.*

It's time for us to learn the song of David. Each believer has been made a king and a priest. Sing Psalm 21 thinking of Father God and "the king." The king is you. The King of kings is Jesus. If He calls us kings and priests we should think differently about this unique title, King of kings and Lord of lords. I always thought of the kings of nations, not the kings in His Kingdom, yet both are true. Adam operated as a king in the Garden of Eden and so should you. Be responsible for what God calls you to do on this earth, for heaven's sake! As we sing Psalm 21, make it our worship to Father God. It is an identity restorer that will take us to our throne of purpose. We can never rest on our crowns, but we must continually roll them towards the throne of our Father in worship so that we continue to wear them for His glory.

When our worship includes our identity as well as our Father God's identity, we have found the *key of David*. It opens doors that no man can shut. *When our worship fully honors our Father God's identity and ours, His life flows through our life.*

David sang his songs of worship to God in the fields and he killed the lion, the bear and eventually Goliath, but he was not ready to take the throne. *When David's worship of God expanded to include his God-given identity, he could now fully rule from the throne of Israel.*